Illumination of the Shadow

Ancestral Wisdom from the
Past for the Future

by
Anthea Durand

Printed in the United Kingdom
First Printing, 2020

Editing: Wendy Yorke.
Design & Typesetting: SWATT Books Ltd.
Cover by Rudi_Design (99Designs)
Illustrations: Tem Casey. IG: @tem_casey.
Email amandocasey@hotmail.com

ISBN: 978-1-8380081-0-9 (Paperback)
ISBN: 978-1-8380081-1-6 (eBook)

Shamanism & Evolving Consciousness Ltd.
www.antheadurand.com

Contents

Dedications

For my mother Maria Guiste, and my father Vaughney Durand, who brought me into being.

For all my ancestors and relations, whose wisdom continues to run through my bones and my soul.

Acknowledgements

I am extremely grateful to my family who have taught me so much about my ancestral lineage. My beloved parents Vaughney Durand and Maria Guiste, for the spiritual gifts of strength, warriorship and love. I am grateful for my three sisters Petula, Josie, and Tina and all my beloved ancestors.

I have immense gratitude to my teacher Tareth, a Master of Alchemy and ancient wisdom, who I have known for many lifetimes. His wisdom, guidance and amazing spiritual teachings helped me to find who I am and to step into my gifts to help humanity.

I would like to thank my beloved friend Sam McCarter who has been a great anchor in my life, a true friend, always there, always supporting. He is a gifted and successful author in his own right, who has always been an incredible friend in all areas of my life, I am grateful for his presence in my life.

I would like to thank Wendy Yorke for her wonderful editing and coaching which helped me to complete this book. She has provided me with strength and direction through the ups and downs of writing this book. Wendy has often gone out of her way to commit to our coaching meetings, in-between her international business travels. I am grateful to Wendy always for helping me to write my first book.

I would also like to thank Samantha Pearce for her wonderful formatting of the book, and for preparing this for self-publication.

I am grateful to Elaku, for all his love, support, and guidance in this lifetime and other lifetimes. I thank all my spiritual teams and ancestors for their love and support.

I also acknowledge and thank the amazing and gifted illustrator Tem Casey, who has provided the powerful and beautiful illustrations for the book, meeting many deadlines and working extremely hard to ensure all were completed.

Thank you to Jacqueline Tobin from Huge Jam publishers for the additional interior proofreading for this book.

I am grateful always to my dear graphic designer Diogo Linhares, who provided the graphic design work for my ancestral courses, which helped birth the ideas for this book.

Special thanks to Professor Julia Kovas, Professor of Genetics and Psychology at Goldsmiths, for meeting me on a one-to-one basis and supporting me with her wisdom about genetics. She has also provided useful advice for my future work to commission scientific studies to prove the influence of ancestral healing on gene behaviour.

Special thanks to all my friends and contributors who have given their time and support to this book. I am eternally grateful to Debora Figueira, Francisco Pereira, Trevor Collom, Judy Lynn-Taylor, Inga Vareva, Susan Morrish, Shozab Khan, Teresa Ribeiro, Olena Hladkova, Clare Vertigan, Christopher Triplett, Nanette Sandiford, Alice Dolle Nicol, Marie Alvarado. Minas Nakhnoukh, Zelda Anne Pritchard, Matleena Nene Kurronen, Jean-Paul Blommaert, Louise James, Rhys Holmes, Marianna Kelly, Victoria Dinham and Lucy Hooper.

I also acknowledge all my students and clients who have supported my work and who have inspired me to develop further healing methods, workshops, and books to help humanity.

Foreword

"Over the last few decades, I have watched Anthea Durand grow in confidence and stature within the spiritual field, so it is no surprise that she has sought to reveal her experience and knowledge in this welcome publication. Her first book, **Illumination of the Shadow; Ancestral Wisdom from the Past for the Future**, transcends the realities of ancestral fields, the realm of shadows, and the present world, and in so doing, seeks to heal the past and the present.

Anthea's book is inspirational and enlightening in an area where there is little else that is comparable. The title of Anthea's book itself is inspiring, resonating as it does with the increasing interest in and awareness of and the impact of ancestral healing and the importance of shadows, and their world. Anthea's writing style is light and easy, drawing the reader along an informative path that weaves the world of our ancestors into our own lives. She successfully shows the significance of the former by shedding a light on the shadows that influence our modern-day reality.

Those people who share Anthea's obvious passion for helping other people through spirituality and shamanism, will find her enlightened thoughts on ancestral and generic healing – as well as family ancestral stories – to be of enormous help and very appealing.

The narrative throughout the publication ten chapters is driven by Anthea's practical experience of real-life ancestral narratives from her own work in both individual and groups sessions, and also by practical steps that have sought to heal the ancestral and shadow realities. Topics range from: Our Ancestral Fields of Existence: Pathways of Consciousness (Chapter 1); to Entities; Manifestations of the Shadows (Chapter 4); and ultimately to, Gifts from the Ancestors; and Celebrations of Divine Inheritance (Chapter 10).

Even for those people who have a passing interest in the field, Anthea's book will inform, inspire illuminate, and hopefully heal."

Sam McCarter, 2019

Sam McCarter has a well-established writing career spanning academic, education and medical fields, and is highly respected in his field. His teaching career spans a period of more than 30 years, starting in Sierra Leone in West Africa as a volunteer. He is a prolific writer, with more than thirty publications, ranging from books to apps. He has been published by the Oxford University Press and Macmillan. He has also written numerous articles on academic and Medical English, as well as being a Consultant Editor in the field of Tropical Medicine. For most of his career he has taught health professionals, mainly doctors. His IELTS app was the winner of the English Speaking Union President's Award in 2013. Website www.internationalenglishlab.com

Praise

"I really enjoyed learning from a book with so much knowledge, which made me reflect about life, ancestors, traumas, emotions and society. The content is very rich and the examples complement each other well. I recommend this book to anybody who is interested in his or her emotions and suffers from any strange illness/behaviours. Also, anyone who is interested in society, in life and healers."

Francisco Pereira, Senior IT Specialist, Mobile App Developer

"Anthea beautifully describes ancestral healing in an easy to understand way, as an ancestral healer and shadow worker myself, I can really relate to what she has written. Ancestral healing is not an easy topic to talk about, let alone write about, so I am really impressed with the style and ease in reading this book. Also, I love the illustrations, they provoke a lot of thought for me and balance the rich content. They clearly express the real emotions and trauma that these poor souls suffered. There are not enough books like this, and I am truly thankful that Anthea has now put this right. This book will go a long way to helping the reader understand ancestral healing in a more profound way. I will recommend this book to my friends and clients, who I am sure would be interested and I know they will benefit from reading it."

Trevor Collom, Ancestral Healer and Direct Marketing Executive for MIND, the United Kingdom's registered mental health charity

"I really enjoyed reading this book and the clear way in which it was presented. It has been quite matter-of-fact reading rather than speculation and vague comments, which tend to accompany esoteric topics. I really liked the authority the author took up while presenting this material. I think having an understanding of the basic energy structure and function of the earth is key, as well as how the earth holds ancestral pain, especially to those

of us who are light workers and who have contracted to help with planetary ascension, then the information in this book is essential. In general, this kind of information is fragmented and is variable, and it is time the information became standardised and streamlined to whatever degree is possible. To this end, this book will be invaluable."

Dr Shozab Khan, General Practitioner

"This excellent book is an ultimate handbook for every ancestral healer and any person who wants to heal any patterns in their lives. It answers many questions which people have had no answers to for a very long time. May this book generate lots of light and help to evolve the planet! Thank you for giving this to the humanity! Congratulations Anthea!"

Inga Vareva, Project Manager, Latvian Literature

"Anthea Durand has studied and experienced shamanic ancestral healing deeply. The book demonstrates the power of thoughts and feelings that move forward in time until they are identified and released. She has created and taught methods that have helped people heal themselves and their ancestral lineage. Her passion to share and teach other people to facilitate healing fills her book. I really enjoyed the detail brought to the subject of ancestral healing and found the case histories very informative. I certainly will recommend this book to people interested in the shamanic healing modalities."

Judy Lynn Taylor, Shamanic Practitioner, Clinical Hypnotherapist, Adventures in Shamanism; blending modern and ancient techniques for healing of spirit

The Author

London-based Anthea Durand BA (Hons), DIP MGT, is an international Spiritual Teacher, Shamanic Practitioner, Alchemist, and Non-Fiction Writer. She has a diverse background including, 20 year's experience as a Senior Manager in Social Housing. Her qualifications include BA Honours in Social Sciences; Postgraduate Diploma in Management; and she is a qualified Trainer. She has travelled the world extensively training and spending time with indigenous people and western teachers, including in: Africa; America; Hawaii; Nepal; Guatemala; Mexico; and Sweden.

She is a gifted channel who channels directly from the source to aid humanity's evolution and healing. She is also a pioneer of Ancestral Healing Practitioner training and other channelled work. She has trained thousands of students to be healers and teachers. She has helped many clients to heal ancestral patterns, connect to their spiritual gifts, and to step into their magical gifts. Anthea is an expert in ancestral healing and she is extremely passionate about this subject and has had meetings with prominent Genetic Scientists at Goldsmiths University, London, United Kingdom, as part of her research into this subject. She intends to commission a scientific study in the future, using the theme of epigenetics to show the influence of ancestral healing on gene behaviour.

Her work is ever evolving and is aligned with the evolutionary energy of the earth. She constantly births new ideas for workshops to help individual and planetary evolution. She produced an album, available on Amazon during 2018, entitled *"Sounds are Awakening"*. Her first book is based on her pioneering work, which delves into the different aspects of the ancestral shadow and it's influence on everyday life. This includes real life ancestral stories, some from thousands of years ago, which illuminate the origin of a problem in the ancestral field.

Ancestral Stories

The ancestral stories discussed in this book have been used with permission and the names of the clients have been altered to ensure confidentiality.

Chapter 1
- Meeting the medicine woman self
- Slave master
- Time in the deepest depths of darkness

Chapter 2
- Grandmother Turtle
- Sword of truth story
- Soul release

Chapter 3
- Depression
- Fear of stepping into one's own power
- Mental illness

Chapter 4
- Panic attacks and fear
- Constantly feeling stuck
- Poor relationship with parents
- Suicidal tendencies
- Alcohol addiction
- Distraught nightmares
- Smoking

Chapter 5

- Ancestral displacement
- Not feeling seen by other people
- Feeling trapped

Chapter 6

- Mother daughter relationship
- Family trauma at time of birth
- Father daughter relationship

Chapter 7

- Wanting to be superior to other people
- Constantly judging oneself and other people
- Other people putting me in danger

Chapter 8

- Alcoholism
- Parkinson's disease
- Anxiety disorder

Chapter 9

- Ukraine and matriarchal society
- Channelled wisdom from the Aboriginal collective
- Channelled wisdom from the Native American collective

Chapter 10

- Gift of healing, mother's side
- Healer with sounds, mother's side
- Master Alchemist, father's side
- Mediumship, mother's side

Illustrations

Chapter 1
- Ancestral field of existence
- Star ancestors
- Doorway to the field of the eternal mind

Chapter 2
- Female Warrior
- Grandmother Turtle
- Sword of truth

Chapter 3
- Magician
- Round table
- Dragon

Chapter 4
- Shaman healing
- Entities
- Negative elementals

Chapter 5
- Slavery collective trauma
- Ancestral displacement
- Freed from chains of slavery

Chapter 6
- Individual trauma
- Shadow Mirror
- Painting with sound

Chapter 7

- Thoughts drive our reality
- Alchemist
- Shaman

Chapter 8

- Ancestral burden
- Spirit of the snake
- Alchemy healer

Chapter 9

- Aboriginal power
- Ukraine sisterhood
- Native American

Chapter 10

- Gifts of wisdom
- Sound healer
- Master Alchemist

Introduction

By Healing your suffering, you help heal the world

The process of illuminating the shadow aids soul healing and evolution. Healing ancestral patterns is the key to unlocking shadow work. As more souls embody more of their source energy on Earth, delving into the shadow is more important than ever. Such delving frees us from energy and patterns that do not serve us anymore. In these turbulent times, the shadow is staring us in the face on an individual and collective level; hence the need to complete this work. The book shares pioneering knowledge and wisdom about the shadow and ancestral healing work.

The process of illuminating the shadow provides access to the gold; the healing and the wisdom within, which are the secrets of the universe ready to be accessed. Healing these secrets brings more joy into your life, along with improved relationships with your family and everyone around you. It provides a deep and safe exploration, through all the ancestral layers, that holds the key to our healing. Our own shadow often manifests itself as an opportunity to delve into the shadow and to find the story behind what is causing us pain.

This book reveals a new and pioneering approach to ancestral and shadow work, pioneered through my own healing and teaching practice, which has been proved to have profound results for healing and transformation.

This publication takes you through an exciting journey, based on shamanic and alchemical practices. The experiences you receive from reading the book are golden insights, which will reveal how your experiences do not start with you. They are interconnected with the complex web of our ancestors and the different ancestral fields feeding into this.

Each chapter provides powerful information about the ancestral fields and provides beautiful illustrations to demonstrate different parts of the ancestral stories that unfold to describe the origin of a problem. The book starts by discussing the Ancestral Fields of Existence, and all the different energetic fields feeding into the ancestral fields, such as: Collective Trauma, Entities, and Thought Forms. Every chapter delves deep into how each field has created a distortion to humanity's source collective, and consequently has created problems for humans, in terms of illness and repeated patterns. In each chapter, profound stories are shared showing how there are many ancestral stories waiting to be heard within us all. Delving deep within ourselves and going back through the origins of time, we can reveal that everyone is from one common ancestor, an ancestor at a time before the love among humanity was lost.

This book is my contribution to shine my light on the ancestral field so the shadows can be lifted from the individual and the collective consciousness. Thus, love, peace and harmony can be restored to humanity.

I studied a Degree in Social Sciences and trained as a Counsellor. I worked as a Manager in social housing for more than 20 years, where I worked tirelessly to help communities and to improve lives on council estates. Daily, I was face to face with many people living in poverty and with many social problems. During this time, I began to connect with spiritual practices, such as Reiki and Meditation. I began to travel extensively around the world, including to: Africa; America; Hawaii; Nepal; Guatemala; Mexico; and Sweden, training in alchemic and shamanic practices with spiritual teachers and indigenous people. These learnings opened my heart and helped me to connect with my spiritual gifts. I felt a calling to follow my spiritual path, so I left my corporate job and followed my heart. I trained as a Reiki Master, a Shamanic Practitioner and in Alchemy. Now, I am a Spiritual Teacher with more than 15 years of experience training students in shamanism, alchemy and pioneering spiritual practices. The trigger to develop ancestral healing practices was a connection I made during a shamanism journey to the Mexican desert. There, the shaman informed me: 'I am here to help dead people'. My heart told me this was connected to ancestral healing and my spiritual journey began to enhance this connection.

I began to research ancestral healing, looking at what was available in the world and I realised there were not many ancestral healers around. I was guided to teach and pioneer methods relating to Ancestral Healing and later, I developed an Ancestral Healing Practitioner Training. My in-depth studies enhanced my knowledge of spiritual practices and enhanced my connection to my spiritual teams and channelling abilities for ancestral work. This book is a combination of years of studies, research, and teaching; a strong connection with my spiritual teams; and the direct channelling of sacred wisdom. I have channelled the information about the ancestral fields, such as: Collective Trauma, Illness, and Thought Forms. I discuss how these are passed down generations, and I provide information on how we can track the origin of a problem and heal it, to help present and future generations.

Every person has their own unique imprint from their ancestors. This book inspires you to unravel your own. Where did the addiction or the illness start? What happened in the ancestral field to your parents' ancestors? What is the story behind this?

The book also provides practical and safe exercises to help you with ancestral healing and to enhance your life. Every chapter summarises and provides profound ancestral wisdom, which you can use in your everyday life. You will gain insights about how you can be motivated and inspired to resolve long-standing ancestral problems, which exist in your own ancestral lines.

I take you through a powerful journey of channelled and researched information, regarding the shadows within the ancestral fields. This journey informs and provides individual resonance with all that is discussed. We are all connected and we often have similar stories and experiences. Healing is provided in this book through the written word and the exercises. Looking into our own and our ancestors' shadows is the key to: healing; spiritual evolution; and personal development. In the shadows are the secrets and the stories that are ready to be heard and told.

Accessing this shadow, while challenging, provides the keys to healing and evolution. In these chaotic times on Earth, there are common experiences that affect all human beings. This book helps to highlight them and give readers insight and peace, knowing they are not alone with their experiences, neither are their ancestors. Shadow work is the energy of now and ancestral work is the doorway.

The underlying principle of this book is to show and demonstrate that ancestral work is the key to transforming what has gone before into something better for future generations. Not only does ancestral work have a profound healing effect on an individual, it also contributes to healing collectives of souls. For example, during one ancestral healing journey, a client had problems with depression. Divination showed this was connected to an ancestor who was affected by slavery and the trauma of this continued through the generations. During the healing process a collective of souls, who had also been slaves at the same time of this ancestor and consequently affected by the same trauma, were also healed and freed from the trauma. Therefore, the impact of this ancestral healing was immense. This healing helped a huge collective of souls and their thousands of ancestors to be freed of the trauma, as well as the client with depression.

We cannot escape our ancestors; their energy is in our bones and our blood. We obtain their gifts, as well as their challenges. Imagine the ability to track back thousands of years to the origin of a repeated illness or pattern that is experienced by you and your ancestors, generation after generation. I demonstrate using my experience and the powerful work of ancestral healers that this is possible. Ancestral healers connect to the origin of a problem and obtain the ancestral stories of what created the illness or pattern in the first place. From connecting to the origin, the client receives healing to free themselves and all the affected ancestors from this issue, forever. The power of this collective healing is that future generations in this ancestral lineage will not suffer with this illness or pattern. The aim of this process is also to bring back ancestral storytelling, much of which has been lost. Passing ancestral stories on orally has not always continued through the generations. These fascinating ancestral stories are healing, empowering and, importantly, they connect us with our ancestors. It serves everyone to pass these stories on to future generations.

Imagine a world where everyone has access to all the stories of your ancestors, this would help you to connect to your lineage, heal relationships, and enable these stories to be passed to future generations. For example, in this book I discuss a family with a history of Parkinson's Disease across many generations. The ancestral healer tracked the origin of the illness to a time in Africa, when an ancestor witnessed the death of her brother, who was bitten by a snake. This caused the essence of this trauma to manifest in Parkinson's disease for future generations, until the time came for it to be reviewed by the ancestral healer, who cleared and healed it for all future generations in the lineage.

I delve into all the different ancestral fields of existence that can create distortion in the human's energy fields, or changes in the DNA, such as collective and individual traumas which affect future generations. This information creates awareness, which not only transforms lives; it also contributes to a shift of consciousness on the planet, which can impact on many generations and the source collective. Humanity has created much of the shadow that exists: individuals and their ancestors need to heal from this.

Ancestral healing and shadow work has been a fascination for me for many years. I have always loved ancient wisdom and how this helps with modern day living. In this book, I also discuss the wisdom of ancestral work from indigenous cultures, alongside my own channelled work to embed modern day ancestral healing practices. Past knowledge and wisdom are not dated; they provide the foundation for the future. It is important to build on the strong foundations of work that already have been achieved by our ancestors. This is how pillars of information are built. Ancestral wisdom, healing, and connection have been a tradition in indigenous cultures for thousands of years. There has been increasing interest in this area and a respect for indigenous traditions by the West, although many are being threatened and lands taken over. I write about different indigenous methods that are used to connect with ancestors, and the methods of healing that are used by traditional healers to heal ancestral issues.

Ancestral healing is relevant to everyone in every moment in time. We all have our own ancestral stories. Many people have problems with repeated patterns, or from trauma in their ancestral fields; it is what makes us human. Conscious awareness is activated by reading this book. An individual experience is also a collective experience, one feeds into the other. This book discusses how individual experiences create an effect, which influences future generations. There is a growing interest among scientists in this area. Scientists write about epigenetics and how a trauma can influence gene behaviour, which continues through the generations. They have discovered how a parent's experience, for example, of a big trauma in their life, can be passed to future generations. I have also consulted with genetic scientists with the aim of commissioning future scientific studies on the impact of ancestral healing on gene behaviour.

By reading this book, you will gain insights and knowledge into indigenous practices around ancestral work, ancestral healing practices, shadow work, and how you can connect more with your ancestors for healing and support. I hope this book inspires you to take the steps to unravel your own ancestral stories.

Energetic work is powerful work and, as demonstrated in this book, you will be inspired by the work that ancestral healing can do to heal and transform.

Ancestor Connection

The seen and unseen
The ancestors are everywhere
There is nowhere to hide
But to embrace that within
From the unseen world the ancestors will call your name
To claim the gifts that are yours
With love and support
Always in the heart
In love and peace
Forever yours.

Chapter 1

Our Ancestral Fields of Existence: Pathways of Consciousness

From the stars to the shadows, from the soars to the lows, from the hope and the despair, the ancestors embrace you.

The Field

The ancestral field is a vast oasis, which extends far beyond the immediate bloodline; it is above us and below us. There are many fields to discuss and explore because the souls and ancestors reside in many fields of existence. It is the loss of connection that creates disharmony. It is the remembrance of the connectedness, which enables more harmony with all of creation because everything is connected. Modern DNA tests have opened the eyes of many people that our origins extend far beyond what we know, connecting the individual to various different cultures, which they would not even think of. Our ancestors have taken many passageways that enable us to be here today. This includes the ancestors who have lived on the earth, those who are connected to the stars, and those who dwell in the shadows, along with those lost in time. Judgement creates a disconnection from what can be learnt and transformed from the ancestors. Moving into our own soul timeline will reveal times when we ourselves have moved through different fields for our own evolution. Spiritual evolution comes with many challenges, highs and lows because moving through the shadow brings realisations.

Contained within each field are particular frequencies that stage a dynamic of association with those souls who align with this. These particular frequencies are encoded with information that is also passed down the generations. They have an impact on the ancestral field, positively and negatively, but all are to be learnt from. There are imprints in many lands where the ancestors have walked as part of their soul journey, for their own individual soul evolution, or to help the planetary evolution. Those who walked the land before, aided where the ancestor is today. Energy holds information, and information is in the land of our ancestors. There have been many journeys as an individual and as part of a collective in different fields of existence. On these journeys there have been waves of peaceful journeys and waves of trauma. The field extends and connects memory of what has been before. It helps to focus different missions and awareness. The soul has an individual journey, but the influence of ancestors is inescapable. Often an individual can carry the burden of the ancestors, particularly if the ancestors choose an ancestor to clear particular patterns that have continued down the generations. It calls you, moves you, challenges you and moulds you. It is an energy that triggers you, whether you like it or not. It is part of your creation.

Many ancestral stories are unknown or hidden within the various ancestral fields. However, ancestral healing provides a great opportunity to reconnect with those stories and to reconnect with this stream of consciousness.

Meeting the Ancestral-Self

In past lives there can be part of the self which has played out in the ancestral journey as the ancestral-self. This needs to be healed and cleared, if it is having a negative impact on the individual or ancestor. When the ancestral-self manifests in a certain time line of the soul, it is to give a focus to a side of a story that is unfinished. For example, Tony might be the son of Martha in one lifetime and return in another lifetime as the mother of Martha. These are often karmic relationships for our learning and evolution. The returning soul often meets whom he or she knows. The ancestral soul is fuel for the ancestors, it ignites or diminishes and it contributes positively or negatively. Engagement acts to fix the lines that have been broken by the manifestation of repeating patterns, which have caused trauma and distress to the self and other people. The soul often chooses a family they have a past connection with. The past life journey is pinpointed to a time when an ancestral pattern needs to be healed. Within our souls are memories of the ancestral field we are connected to. As part of the ancestral journey, the ancestral-self may need to complete many lifetimes of meeting and healing with their own ancestors, until a repeated pattern is healed. We are part of the learning that fuels our existence and we need to take responsibility for our role in the ancestral field.

Ancestral Story
Meeting the medicine woman self

The ancestral healer worked with Samantha. After opening the space and calling in her spirit guides, she proceeded to journey to find the origins of any trauma affecting Samantha in her current life. The first image she saw were lots of wolves running; they seemed really angry and upset. The environment was a forest or jungle, with lots of green space. She saw the backs of people running away trying to save themselves. However, within this space was a light, as the sun was shining through a space in the trees, there was a woman holding a small male child. As the ancestral healer progressed through the journey, she realised that the wolves were protecting the woman and child. In the distance was a mast and sails, danger was coming and there were intruders invading the land. The wolves started to chase the invaders away while also protecting the woman and child.

The feelings were that this woman was left with a huge responsibility because she had to look after the child and she was left alone. There was a sense of loneliness and the immensity of this huge weight of responsibility that she carried not only for this child, but also for her village. While the ancestral healer was giving healing to Samantha, she felt the presence of an African Shaman who helped clean up and remove the negative energy from Samantha. As the ancestral healer shook a rattle and gave healing, it felt like a huge integration of herself and she described it as a magical experience.

A week after the session, Samantha had a past life regression session. She found herself in a forest in the Caribbean. She had a little hut for a home and a fire outside in front of her hut. On the fire was a pot of herbs brewing. She went deeper into the forest and felt so connected to the plants and herbs. The pot brewing was medicine she was making for people in her village. She was a medicine woman of St. Lucia. It was through this experience that she realised she was one of her ancestors, returning to the family in this lifetime from St Lucia, with the gifts that she had inherited.

Working with the ancestral-self encourages personal growth and realisation. There are many circumstances that show themselves for healing of the ancestral-self, at the appropriate time. Every soul has been the reverse of what they have been before. The reversal creates the formula to embed that which allows the soul to stride forward, in the evolving direction of the soul's evolution.

The ancestral-self can be the pioneer, which helps liberate many people in their own field; returning as the ancestral-self provides that opportunity. They can also provide strength to ancestors in the field who are suffering in turmoil. The liberation of ancestors, whose souls have been distorted by misery and pain, can be a role of an ancestral-self. Carrying the burden of the ancestors is hard work, but transforming this is rewarded with many spiritual gifts that can transform the individual and many other people. On the negative side, the ancestral-self can add further pain to the ancestral field, which needs to be healed and transformed.

Ancestral Story
Slave master

The ancestral healer completed divination to find out if Mary had inflicted trauma on other people, which was affecting her or her ancestral lineage. She discovered there was a very old curse, which she had inflicted on other people connected to her mother line. She was from a family of slave masters directly involved in the transportation of African slaves from their lands and in charge of shipping channels; she was a male in charge. He was very powerful and frightening and he created fear in the hearts of people with a look or stare. This caused many of his victims to shut down emotionally. He cursed a collective of slaves with his stare and words. His words were so negative and strong that this took the wind out of other people, who could not breathe out of fear. The thought form he created was one of power and financial gain. The money earned through slavery was cursed as blood money. This curse was passed on through his own ancestors and anyone who received or benefited from this money, along with the curse affecting those slaves he had cursed. This curse caused great unhappiness down the ancestral line. Healing was completed to release this from the ancestral field.

Ancestors from The Stars

Scientists recognise that we are all stardust. Our origins also have a connection to the stars energetically and physically. Many people have ancestors directly connected to the stars and many of these ancestors live here on earth. Ancestors from the stars have often incarnated directly on the earth to help the earth with its evolution. There are many star frequencies and different lineages of connection. The stars contain much of the memory of the making of the human form. The human makeup was shaped by intelligence that enabled those who embodied the human form to live easily on the earth. The ancestors from the stars and their lineages hold the energetic makeup of the evolved forms of life. The density of the human body matches that of the density of the earth, so the human form embodies on earth. As the earth evolves, so does the human form evolve and change on earth.

Within each star, are different frequencies of souls. It is well known that souls from the evolved aspect of, for example Sirius B, Orion, Arcturius or Pleiades, have been helping the earth with its evolution for thousands of years. When the wisdom from the star ancestors is tapped into, it is very powerful. It can bring a spark of life to the self, along with helping other people immensely. It is easy to turn away from this idea, associating this connection with the word 'alien', when in fact this concept is not alien to us at all.

Creating a direct link with the ancestors from the stars serves to create balance, harmony and connection with great wisdom. The disconnection can create the feeling of not belonging on Earth, not understanding the self, and detachment from the many gifts, which can be received from the connection to this immense and beautiful energy.

People who have ancestors and origins directly connected to the stars carry immense gifts to help humanity. Many stars, such as Sirius B, have evolved to a frequency that is ahead of the earth, and thus contain wisdom of the future to help the earth. There are many different and amazing spiritual qualities that stars embody for these ancestors to bring to the earth to help others.

Sirius B

Sirius is a binary star and the brightest in the sky. Sirius B is the smaller star and is known as the White Dwarf discovered in the early years of the 20th century. The Dogon tribe from Mali in Africa hold fascinating stories of the connection with star energies as part of their mythology. They have always believed they are an ancient tribe and they are connected to the ancient Egyptians. The Dogon tribe knew of the existence of Sirius B, which the human eye cannot see, before it could be detected by astronomers. It was identified by astronomers in 1862. This baffled astronomers as to how they knew this star existed. The Dogon tribe have a wonderful understanding of the universe along with an understanding the complexities of the universe. They possess a 400-year artefact, which shows the Sirius configuration. As described by Dr Kathy J Forti, in *Infinity and Beyond*, the Dogon tribe believe that: "An earlier race of aliens came to our solar system from Sirius B almost 1,000,000 years ago".

There are many spiritual qualities connected to Sirius B. There is a strong connection to sound; many temples in Sirius B are connected to sound. It is also connected to the divine feminine. There are many people who embody this energy and who complete great work for the earth. The work that is completed on Sirius B acts as a training ground for other souls, and to prepare souls for their time on Earth. The ancient Egyptians held the signature for this star and were able to bring in the pioneering work to help the future. It is also well known that the great pyramid is aligned to the Sirius B star.

Ancestors from Sirius B hold the power of sound. They are able to navigate easily through different aspects of time. They meet to create communities of light and sound within each Sirian starseed. Information is transmitted to help other people drive forward earth consciousness; they have a huge love for the earth. They are able to transmute negative energies easily and are therefore great ambassadors to help the earth evolve. Their drive for change gives a strong focus for their mission. Many ancestral tribes worked with this energy, to help ground them in the frequencies that they embodied. In every Sirius B being is the ability to change matter into energy easily, which cannot be understood by the human mind. They are the holders of many magical practices that can be manifested at will.

Pleiades

The Pleiades are known as the Seven Sisters. The actual star cluster contains more than 400 stars; however, there are seven most visible to the naked eye. The qualities of those ancestors connected to the Pleiades are of unconditional love. They work hard to help the newly-evolved children who are being born on Earth, to be able to integrate well. They have a role in protecting the earth and helping with its evolution.

Native Americans talk about a sacred place in heaven, which they refer to as the Pleiades. The Lakota legends discuss how they originated from the Pleiades and are immigrants from star nations. They believe that after a person dies, the soul of the person will return there. They also state that while they are on earth, they will care for it.

Orion

The Belt of Orion is a very visible constellation throughout the world. The Orion Belt is also known as the Three Kings or Three Sisters. In Orion there are different levels of frequencies. Those ancestors connected to this energy often have the symbology of a golden crown at the top of their heads, symbolic of the vibration of the higher level of the crown chakra. This star energy is connected to alchemy and the gifts of making the shadow visible. Mastery of the shadow is what brings real evolution of the self. By knowing both sides, they are able to help other people to do so, and to heal and transform. Using alchemy to illuminate the dark and transform it, they have the power to embrace both sides of self, leading to the rebirth of the self. They meet in sacred places, holy temples and energetic caves to ensure sacredness. They often wear gowns that cover their whole being for protection and to keep their identity sacred and hidden.

The ancestors from this star often play a significant role for humanity. While they have enormous love for other people, their earthly existence is often the journey of opening the heart as a human on Earth. They cast a shadow of illumination where some people will not venture, which requires courage, resilience and strength. There have been many divisions in the past for those souls connected to the Orion star. This is due to power struggles, because the ancestors of Orion hold very powerful energy. This power, however, holds the gifts of creating great change for other people. The challenge is how those connected to Orion use their power for the good, or if they allow it to get out of hand, causing misery and abuse. Their human struggle has often been to master this power effectively, which often creates a power struggle within the self and other people.

The Orion ancestors hold profound wisdom of everything. There is great sacredness here and much is veiled in secrecy. It is only revealed to those who operate at a similar level, which is given to manifest for the good of all. There is high protection for those humans from Orion, because they have much work to do to help many fields of existence. When these ancestors return to Earth, they often have an important mission for it. Orion offers many skills in wisdom, working with different energies at the same time and the abilities to manifest energies in different forms. They are focused and disciplined and are here to make major changes on the earth. They are associated with Merlin and King Arthur; Alchemy; Dragons; and White Lion Masters.

Fields of Eternal Mind

Does hell exist? Not as people have been informed. However, dwelling in this realm can be a miserable existence. This place does not have to do with reward and punishment as is often described by religion, but residing here is to do with the soul resonance that the soul carries.

There are fields where the mind dominates rather than the heart. These are extremely dense and many souls drift away from the light of their being, and become stagnant on their soul journey. Working constantly from the mind creates a degree of separation, but this can be lifted by connecting to the heart and reflecting on the time when separation did not take place. It is this which needs to be mirrored to those people who are suffering in the depths of despair. Opportunities to move on from this field on the soul journey will always present themselves. No one is forgotten and all souls have a soul guardian.

The movement of time matter is within the soul information, which connects us all and is universal love. It is this simple reconnection, which sets those souls free from a miserable existence. We create separation by judging people who exist here. Many of these souls are our ancestors and they all deserve to be given an opportunity to be shown the light again, and not to be continually in a miserable existence. Judging those souls here is like a mirror image of judging ourselves. This place should be treated with caution because there are many souls who are powerful and are connected to dense dark energies. They can sometimes be intent on continuing to cause harm, and to keep souls stagnated and disconnected from themselves.

There are also higher forces such as Arch Demons that continue to feed into the negative thought forms, thus creating a cycle that the soul cannot get out of. This is the mindset of the surroundings where displaced souls operate within. Souls connect to this dimension via their mindset. There may be ancestors in our own lineage who exist at this level. If they are in our own ancestral field, they can make it problematic for an ancestor to complete their work for the good, particularly if they are completing ancestral work. Of course, this field of existence can attract people who have carried out dark deeds, or have been evil to other people. There could also be souls residing here who have experienced an extremely bad trauma and the weight of their negative thought forms may have carried them to this place. Souls may have lost their way to the light and may have been taken here by the dark energies, which reside here.

This place is full of contradictions and does not operate from love. Contradictions in the sense that the avenue to emerge out of it is often tampered with. Many souls, including many ancestors, can be stuck and blocked in this aspect of reality, stagnated in time. How we exist in different fields is related to our frequency. Each soul is destined to an arrival that suits its frequency. These places are dark because they place what has been created into the appropriate memory. The disharmony creates separation between souls. The energy of the combined souls manifests as darkness.

A frequency has sound, as does each individual soul. In this reality the sounds do not allow for free movement, it weighs the soul down like chains to the floor. It dulls the senses and aids disconnection, often from the souls around them. In this place is the umbrella effect, there are periods when this opens and rays of light are able to enter to give hope. At other times, the umbrella is closed and it is hard to navigate. Every process leads to understanding and reflects back to the soul, until a time when a real opening is given to flow forward in time on their soul journey.

In this field, control is the dominant factor; it does not allow a breathing space other than to exist. With this concept is memory, but memory is tainted by that which is unknown, or has been recovered from memory. Not allowing access to soul memory blocks memory when souls are in this place. They try and create new realities, but it is like trying to plough through dense mud. There are no means of escape other than hoping change will happen. For many souls this existence has played out for thousands of years. It is what they know and are familiar with. It operates within a restricted and confined environment; the dense energy keeps them restricted. The impact of this on the ancestral field is that this stuckness can affect a living ancestor and manifest in various ways. Ancestral healing and therefore the method of tracking the origin of the problem, is one way to heal an individual soul and a collective. However, all souls have soul guardians, who are standing by and guarding the soul; no one is lost.

The problem with this dimension is that it can suck any light out of those souls who dwell there. Help comes in the form of spiritual prayer, healing, and recovery by other people, which happens in all dimensions. Souls who are there can be helped in many ways. They can be shown light to remember who they are and that light does exist. This is a mechanism for them to connect again and to continue their journey. Mass bursts of lights are often shown to help souls continue their journeys, when they have been disconnected from the light for so long. Evolution always takes place on all fields of light. Sunlight shows itself and then disappears on Earth, but humans on earth know the light is coming, but this is not the same for souls who dwell here. Many of our ancestors are here and they all desire a healing journey for the soul. The wall that the ancestors face to their soul evolution can be broken down by a connection to the ancestral lineage, by healing any blockages of connection and sending healing down the ancestral line. The creation of thought forms of many souls in this dimension can continue down the generations; thought forms of fear and control.

Ancestral Story
Time in the deepest depths of darkness

Leon recalled a past life of an experience in the field of the eternal mind. The place was grey. He was a man and there were massive walls wherever he turned, which had no end. When he entered there, his soul went through a dark tunnel, which had no light. The gardens he faced were not of bloom and light, but they were made of cement. The visual senses were dumbed down to connect with this environment. All he felt was pain, physical and emotional and most of the other senses felt like they had been taken away, along with all the feelings he could normally enjoy. He recalled trying to climb the walls with his energetic feet and hands, but the walls were too tall and they seemed to never end. He felt an overwhelming feeling of grief and sadness and he spent an extremely long time there.

He was aware of a female guide who told him he could walk through the wall. She also informed him that he was overwhelmed with grief and pain, and this energy was causing him to disconnect from himself. His female guide began to reconnect him to his source light being, gradually reconnecting him with his heart, and reminding him of the source energy of love. She began teaching him how to move out of this existence. She reminded him that he was a soul and who he was before he lost consciousness of his past. She encouraged him to recover who he was and how he needed to reconnect with that.

He was told he could walk through the wall, back to the source of light. She told him that the walls were energy and porous like her body; if he believed what she was saying, he could move out of this environment. It was imprisoning his soul and he was manifesting himself as a limited being, who could not escape this prison. She said she was sent to help him. She asked him to remember the time he was connected to his heart. When she told him this information, he believed it and reconnected to his heart and he stepped into his soul. He was able to move through the walls and his guide helped him into the light to continue his soul journey.

Middle World

The middle world can look very much like the earth plane, but it can morph in and out of what is true and not true. What you see is not what you get of this reality, and those souls who inhabit it. It is a confused environment with none of the ethics found in the upper and lower worlds. Many souls who die in anger, sudden death, deep grief, can end up in the middle world. It can be a place of great suffering and not a wonderful place to exist in. Some souls enter the middle world on route to the other fields of existence and spend time here for training and being tested. This is not a safe place to explore energetically, or to let down boundaries of protection because the guardians of this place do not always conform to the higher universal laws or benevolence. If healers are exploring this place through their energy bodies, they need to take their guides with them for protection. Many souls can get stuck here; it is full of trickster spirits who pretend to be certain spirits and are not what they appear. They can appear as beams of light when they are not. Everything you see is not a true picture of what reality is.

Many ancestors can be stuck here, as they have not crossed over to the light. Unfortunately, in this field they can be confused and disconnected, lost from who they are and who they have been. On some occasions they can feed into the life force of living people or become entity attachments to maintain themselves. To work with ancestors in this world and other beings who reside here can be dangerous energetically, and healers need to be properly trained to do so.

This is a very transient reality, many ancestors moving onto different fields of existence after a period of time. It is like a rite of passage to learn and go onto the next level, and of various attempts to leave this world. Souls in the middle world go through tests before going to the appropriate level. Many of our ancestors can end up residing there for a while and some ancestors get stuck here.

Earth Field of Existence

Earth provides the foundation for learning, because of its density a variety of souls with a variety of frequencies can reside there. The earth is also on its own evolutionary path. It also calls in those souls who can act as guardians for the earth and who hold a particular vibration to help it to evolve. Many of our ancestors have acted as guardians of the earth and have worked with and created particular spiritual practices, that have helped other souls to embody the light and evolve on the earth. On the earth, blood ancestors show themselves in a human body, which enables the embodiment of the mind, body and spirit and creates the perfect vessel for the availability of connectedness and embodiment of the source.

The earth is the field where we are in physical form, standing side by side with those who are in our ancestral line. There are ups and downs that extend from this relationship, but we choose before we are incarnated to be part of this particular bloodline. There are many ancestral stories from the past that lead to these particular ancestral combinations of love, challenge, and healing. Some ancestors' spirits can remain stuck on the earth for various reasons, for example because of a sudden death, a lost soul, attachment to the earthly life and to the people who inhabit it.

All souls are on a journey. Within the bloodline are different souls at different stages of their soul evolution. All are related, but energetically vibrating at different levels. Some are more connected to the light and some more connected to the dark; others are fragmented by trauma and some are vibrating at a high level. Each soul works out its divine plan before coming to earth; within each soul are divine echoes and sounds. This echo creates sounds that reconnect with those souls who have karmic patterns, and who will create the right sequence to harmonise and manifest the life and learning the soul needs.

The earth ancestors help the individual to achieve their mission, learning and healing. This combination activates what the soul needs. The soul has a choice to listen to the learning and to conquer it, or return to a similar combination of ancestors on the earth to repeat what has not been healed or learnt. The work is to understand the concept of the relationship with the challenging ancestors. What does it show us? What needs to be healed? Of course, along with the many challenges, there are the gifts that also come from the lineage, which enable the soul to achieve their mission. Both are playing out at the same time.

Healing Ritual Exercise

Find a quiet space. Cleanse your space with incense or sage and meditate to create a quiet mind. Light two candles. One candle will represent the ancestors on your father's side and the other will represent your mother's side.

Focus on one candle at a time and connect to your heart. Call in your guides and ancestors for the highest good. Send love, compassion, and peace. Let this radiate out from your heart and connect to both ancestral lines. Intend harmony and light to illuminate the way, for those ancestors who may need your help. Do this in turn to your mother's line and your father's line, and state the ancestor prayer below.

Ancestor Prayer
Shine the light to bring all in harmony
I send unconditional love
I pray that you see this light of love
That this resurrects what you know
A light of source
Free to move on its journey with love and support
Opening the door for you to take flight
Away from the darkness that holds you.
Returning to your eternal light.

Give thanks and blow out each candle to complete the ritual.

Ancestral Wisdom

Ancestors reside in different fields of existence. They can be limited in their soul evolution because they reside in fields that have hindered or stopped their soul evolution. We are not responsible for individual ancestral soul evolution however, sometimes certain ancestors who are stuck in a particular field that can affect a living ancestor, causing a similar pattern or illness. When an ancestor shows up who is residing in this field as part of an individual's healing process, steps can be taken to heal, free, and work with this energy, but only with a properly trained ancestral practitioner.

Freeing ourselves of judgment creates less separation and opens the doors of healing of our ancestors and ourselves. There are of course, ancestors who are not yet able to connect or align with an ancestor and agree to work with dark energies. There are also living ancestors who will use this ancestral wisdom to work with the dark forces here on Earth too. People need to be careful and have awareness of this if it is directly connected to their ancestral lineage and not aligned with the persons frequency, as these ancestors may want to block the positive aspects of the ancestor's soul journey.

We have ancestors connected to the stars and the higher frequencies of light. They extend their wings and wisdom to the ancestors that embody this, to bring great change to other people the planet and all forms of life. These gifts are transmitted to those people who are connected to this to help evolve the future. The number of people who are connected to this ancestral wisdom is growing, as the earth continues its evolution. This paves the way for more of this energy to be embodied in ancestors on the earth. In the sparkles of the stars the ancestral light beams become directives of evolutionary change that is transformative, and enables the embodiment of coded information. This provides a compass and directive of illumination.

We remember those ancestors who are currently disconnected from their souls and light, placed in a wilderness that entangles and stifles what light and remembrance they had. Also, those ancestors who are stuck on their soul journey, confused in a form that has lost its navigation lens. We send hope that the navigation lens returns and allows a tracking so they remember who they are. All souls have guardians with them. All have hope and a divine right to extend their soul light again. We hold them in our hearts and hope that the extended pain diminishes so they can fly again.

Reflection time

*Write your insights, healing and tasks moving
forward to continue to heal your life.*

Chapter 2

Navigating the Ancestral Fields of Existence: Pinpointing and Engineering Change

Movement flows like a cascade of water as we navigate our bloodline to access our eternity.

Navigating the ancestral fields, requires strength, resilience, training, and initiation into energetic processes. It is not for the faint hearted to connect with these powerful fields that hold the shadows, the darkness along with the light. But these fields are full of wisdom, and hold keys of information that can unlock doorways to ancient wisdom and healing. It is no wonder that in order to navigate these fields strong initiations and training with expert teachers are required.

During my teaching and healing practice and training students to be ancestral healers, I have become aware of the tools needed to develop a powerful and safe method, to navigate the ancestral fields to heal other people. It is very important to work safely because the ancestral fields are connected to many aspects of trauma, and many energies that are not aligned to the light. They also contain fields of energies with positive and negative experiences.

I channelled a profound method of ancestral healing. This method empowers and develops the practitioner to pinpoint the origin of the ancestral issue, which can be connected to an issue in a present life, or one from thousands of years ago. Once the origin of the problem is found, the appropriate healing is given to liberate and heal the affected individual and all who are affected by this aspect of consciousness. The focus of the healing is navigating to the origin of the issue, which is having a negative influence on the ancestral lineage. A shamanic initiation into the ancestral field is required to work effectively and safely. This chapter discusses the tools that allow navigation of these fields and why this is important.

Navigating the Ancestral Fields

Navigating the ancestral fields is a big initiation into a consciousness, which feeds into the consciousness of the earth. This should be treated with caution because these fields contain different frequencies of consciousness related to the souls there. Where there is light there is dark; we all learn from each other. These layers of consciousness access cellular memory that offers a profound history of ancestral memory. It links directly to the earth and other planetary and star memories. This also includes memory of collective trauma, the origin of man and memories of man's evolutionary past and present. Accessing this wisdom can elevate consciousness to another level on the earth: for example, the ability to access information on the original blueprint of man, before distortion in the energetic fields occurred. Our ancestors left their imprints in our quantum field of memory to be accessed at the right time, for individual and planetary evolution. This field is an energetic container to learn from the shadow and evolve beyond this, and to be in harmony with the planet and ourselves.

Many of the ancestral fields are connected to the astral plane, along with those connected to higher planes of light: many of our ancestors are also from the stars. The astral plane is a plane of existence that holds a space, where spirits reside in a similar type of earth bond reality, in a frequency that is similar to the one they resided in on

Earth. Some spirits have been stuck in the astral plane for a long time. Contained within the astral plane are also different realms of existence and difference frequencies of souls including entities, therefore connecting with this ancestral field needs particular tools and skills. These tools give the support and protection needed when navigating these fields. For example, some souls may have been stuck in a particular aspect of their consciousness, due perhaps to a lifetime of inflicting harm on other people. As souls they may have become so wrapped up with guilt, they can form into an entity form, detaching more and more from the frequencies of light and love. This energy can have no emotions, and thus dealing with this energy form should be treated with caution and with particular skills that the healer has been trained in using. All souls have different frequencies and a soul resides on the plane of existence, which is in resonance with its frequency. Through the ancestral bloodline we are connected to different frequencies of souls. The key is to connect with the ancestral collective or soul that is affecting us in this lifetime and to heal and harmonise that which no longer serves us.

Sounds of the soul connect particular frequencies of souls together. A soul is connected to thousands of ancestors, many holding great light and we can also learn from them. They are supporting us every day on our journey here on Earth. The web of the ancestors has a direct influence on the consciousness of the earth and it is a complex web. This consciousness has left an imprint in the universe and is feeding in on all levels into the consciousness of Earth, a huge and fascinating area to explore. We are bound together by our bloodlines; because of this we have shared ancestral spirits. However, we remain in resonance with those which match our frequency. In the universe there is no separation, we are all one family, one source. We can say that humanity is also intrinsically linked together with the ancestral fields; a cosmic world wide web of ancestors.

A skilled and gifted ancestral practitioner can complete amazing healing work. However, it is important that they access the right energetic tools, which support and empower, so that the ancestral field can be navigated safely. The ancestral fields of existence can be accessed safely and easily, with the empowered-self and spiritual teams to assist. Contained within these ancestral fields are similarities common to mankind; a time consortium mirror reflecting energetic distortions and thought forms in the collective. These may have been caused by a number of factors including trauma, displacement or other factors outlined in this book. Within every individual is an aspect of self that has been affected in some way by a link with an ancestor and the collective shadow. In these collective fields there is much gratitude for ancestral memory that we can access and many ancestors are waiting for this information to be accessed on their behalf. The evolution of the soul is directly linked to the evolution of the planet, so we can access memories both positive and negative to aid our soul journey.

A situation or action can create a distortion in the ancestral field and subsequently to an individual soul. This distortion causes a distortion in a soul's connection to the earth, creating disharmony. Ancestral work is important for the real evolution of the self and the planet. Disconnection in the ancestral field is causing disharmony in humanity; and much of humanity has lost its connectedness with nature and with each other. The ancestors want their stories to be heard. These stories are soul enriching, they are stories to tell our ancestors about how an ancestral trait manifested. There are many stories that need to be heard from the ancestors and they want to share them. From feeding these stories into the collective, we can reconnect humanity with their lineage and their wisdom and gifts, which is part of their inheritance. This also raises awareness and helps to connect to the reasons as to why disharmony has occurred in the ancestral fields. For example, if we knew all the lands that we are connected to in different lifetimes and all the different creeds and colours we have been, would there still be discrimination and would we become more liberal in our thinking? The importance of conveying this information via divination is important, not only for the individual but for the collective. It is time for everyone on the earth to love and live back together in harmony.

Spiritual Allies

Ancestral Gatekeepers

Accessing the spokesperson for the amazing ancestral web is important. There are ancestors who are vibrating at a particular frequency; we call these souls gatekeepers to the ancestral fields. Healers ask them to step forward as negotiators on behalf of the ancestors. These ancestral gatekeepers are able to effectively hold all energies of the ancestral fields simultaneously and easily, in the subtle timeline of reality. They communicate on behalf of the ancestors through an amazing cosmic web. All is right in the divine timing of the client who has stepped forward to receive the healing, and so is the ancestral link that is ready to be freed from the energetic chains that have bound them in a distorted aspect of time.

Spiritual Teachers

A strong connection with a spiritual guide is imperative to receive information and guidance about a problem. In indigenous cultures, the medicine person will work directly with the spirits to receive guidance. In many traditions, divination takes place directly with the ancestors for advice and support. For example, in the African Swazi tradition divination is carried out by direct communication with the ancestors. At the centre of Swazi divination is the Sangoma who is possessed by the ancestors. From this connection communication with the ancestors takes place and the Sangoma communicate the answers to help locate what is hidden to resolve a problem for the client.

In the method I have developed of ancestral healing, I have been guided that ancestral practitioners should work directly with a spiritual teacher. I teach students to connect to these guides during a shamanic initiation. The spiritual teacher for ancestral work acts as the connector between the ancestral spirits of the client and the ancestral healer, so information can flow to the healer that will help the client. The spiritual teacher acts as a focus for the central issues. The spiritual teacher is energetically aware and connected to the ancestral spirits, and to the negotiations and communications in the ancestral fields. Negotiations relate to the coded information that is transferred from one ancestor to another, via the connection to the gatekeeper. The spiritual teacher is able to communicate on all levels, connected to the energy of the healer and the information is transferred during the divination process.

An initiation into finding the spiritual teacher is an important process. A shamanic journey takes place to find the spiritual teacher for ancestral work in the upper world. There are many ancestral stories of the powerful energy of spiritual teachers who practitioners have connected to and some of these stories are featured in this chapter.

The Bone Man Story

A practitioner connected with her spiritual teacher, who she named the Bone Man. This guide is a very wise teacher who acts as the earth's record keeper and he holds the stories of the earth and of those people who lived on earth. She was shown that these stories are recorded on leaves that he looks after. During divination and healing work, the Bone Man helped her to connect to the earth's records for the individual and the collective. He is connected to all the ancestral stories that exist, to help heal other people.

Ancestral Story
Grandmother Turtle

A student had a guide called Grandmother Turtle. She appeared as an old lady with long greyish hair, deep black eyes and on her back, she wore a turtle shell. Her eyes were dark and as deep as lakes. As the healer connected with and entered her teacher's eyes, it appeared as if she was in a place of no time. This guide had shown her the inside of her shell. Inside the shell was a map of a net of light and within that light was information regarding the ancestors. By looking at this map she was able to see and hear gaps of distortion. When working with this guide, the healer heard the words of encouragement from the guide; "Weave it and make it whole". Also, "Make it strong". This guide also advised that the sound can be used to open the web to the ancestors and to call in the ancestors in need of healing, and use sound for closing the session and grounding. The practitioner has worked closely with this guide with amazing results for her clients.

The Female Warrior Story

A female Scandinavian warrior going back many generations, very fierce and a powerful warrior presented herself as a guide for an ancestral healer. This guide stopped any negative energy coming close to him and she was very protective. When she worked with him during the ancestral work, she carried a sword of light that worked to heal and was also to protect.

The spiritual teachers are the divine witnesses and helpers: the more we work with them, the stronger the connection will be and the better and more accurate information can flow; this is important in ancestral work. Having a spiritual guide and a very close connection to this guide is imperative for this work.

Tools of Power

Tools of power aid the healing session in magical ways. They protect and help to transform our reality. They are energetic tools that are familiar and are aligned with the soul frequency of the person who connects with this. I initiate ancestral healers into receiving their tools of power, to help them energetically step more into their own power and also to help to create a protective space when completing ancestral work.

Shamans in the physical world also work with many magical tools, which form part of their healing practice. Some shamans use drums, rattles and have magical shamanic objects. In the Zulu tradition in Africa, the Sangoma hold a wildebeest tail to summon the spirits. Sometimes white beads are worn in the hair, to stop any evil spirits entering the hut where they are working. As described by the author Barbara Tyrrell, in her book, *Suspicion Is My Name*, there are necklaces worn by witchdoctors, which consist of two types of medicinal seeds. These are alternated black and white and the seeds act as a strong defence against evil spirits. Physical energetic tools are common across many shamanic traditions. They also can act as antennae for spirits and have magical properties, along with being extremely protective.

These tools of power that I initiate ancestral healers into connecting with are magical objects, which are connected to the frequency of the person who works with them and are energetically transported to the physical world, by being invoked by the mind of the healer. These enable the navigation of the ancestral fields powerfully and easily. They also help the transformation of the holder to be more in their energetic power. These source tools are already connected to the healer on an energetic level and also they help the healer to step more into their magical power. The tools of power also hold ancient wisdom of the person who connects with them and they help with the manifestation of their source abilities on Earth. Magical tools such as these enable the healer to move into different aspects of time simultaneously.

Ancestral Story
Sword of truth tool

The ancestral healer connected to her tool of power, a sword of truth. This was a matte silver sword with the alchemical symbol of the rose in the centre of the cross guard. She was informed it would glow gold when used. It is the user's responsibility to ensure that the sword is used for the highest good. This sword is forged in fire and contains the flame of spirit. It represents strength, discrimination, intellectual power, courage, authority and control. It is the weapon of the Knight band, which can be used to battle and to defend and to bless. It is an alchemical weapon. It contains all the elements, metal and minerals from the earth and is forged in fire, cooled in water, conceived through the mental processes of air, the intent of the smith. This is a powerful tool, that helps her in her healing practice.

A Black Bluish Stone Tool

An ancestral healer connected to her tool of power, which was a black, bluish stone, translucent and full of stars and galaxies. The spiritual stone connected to the owner helping her to focus and protect herself when completing ancestral work. The stars are important because they are our ancestors too; the stone reminds us that we are all made of stardust. This tool of power moved the user into a no time position, when she could visualise the web of creation and how we are all ultimately connected. She also felt that her soul origin was in the stars and this stone also helped her to connect with this aspect of herself.

Many of these tools of power are related to the ability to navigate time. Some of these tools show themselves as energetic crystals that access the time reality and connect and track the origin of the problem. The tools of power aid the healing session in magical ways helping to transform our reality. These are invoked energetically by the mind to aid the divination process, along with empowering the healer during a session.

Magical Altars

An altar is a structure that provides a focus for ritual. It also acts as a portal to create a safe space for healing work to take place. For ancestral healing work, I was guided to develop an altar that would enable different pathways of energies that were connected to the healer to be opened to create a powerful space. This serves two purposes: firstly, it provides an energetic space of protection; and secondly, it empowers as it opens more gateways in the energetic fields that the healer is connected to and to more spiritual allies. The healers call in frequencies that they are aligned with and this allows more of their source self to be present, not only during the healing sessions, but also in their own physical bodies. It is a powerful initiation and one that leads to more powerful personal power to complete this work.

The altar works by using four stones or crystals. Each represent fire, earth, water or air. We always start with air in the energetic north, walk around in a clockwise position to fire in the east, earth in the south and water in the west. In alchemy terms to really evolve on our soul journey, we need to be at one with the elements and aligned with these four aspects of consciousness. The elements are a living consciousness, which are part of us. They communicate and open doorways to our magical-self.

The altar serves different expressions. Air opens the doorway to freedom of expression; fire to soul liberation; earth to the structure of the soul; and water to the self and soul memory.

To activate this alchemical altar, you can meditate on each element or use a rattle or drum when calling these in. Start with air and walk round in a clockwise direction, to fire, earth and water. For each element complete the following important ritual:

1. Call in the element.
2. Call in your animal guide for that element.
3. Call in your angelic guide for that element.

4. Call in your star guide for that element.
5. Call in your dragon guide for that element.

If you do not receive a clear image or guide only connect to the energy that is brought forth. For example many people will not connect to a star guide or dragon guide that is acceptable. However, be aware that not all energies will connect with you. Write down the details of your guides in each of the element directions. Walk around in a clockwise direction calling the guides for each element until completed. This process provides a strong protective space for ancestral work and it is also empowering as you open up more to your source-self. For each of the elements you call in the different aspects above. If you do not receive any information regarding all the guides, which can happen, you will call in the guides you have connected to. However, at the minimum, there should be a connection to an animal guide and the elements, air, fire, earth and water, which form a strong foundation for this altar and create a strong energetic space. After opening the altar always remember to close down. To close the altar, start with the element of air, stand with your back to air and thank this element. Walk around in a clockwise direction and complete this with the other elements. If any energies come through that you do not feel comfortable with, disconnect from that energy.

There have been many magical changes that have taken place when students have opened an altar in this way, as this is a source altar to self, and therefore this helps you on your soul journey. For example, a healer I trained acknowledged that after opening his altar he experienced powerful dragon guides in all directions. He advised that after opening the altar using his rattle, he was startled by the new power and energy that started to come through. The altar has helped him to connect with his source-self and his powerful energies and gifts. The altar is a portal to opening all to the source divine-self on Earth. Such empowerment is important for ancestral work and for empowering the soul journey.

Altar Components

Fire

This converts and transforms. It operates by liberating that which no longer serves us. Fire shines a light like an eternal flame. Its powerful energy helps clear away anything that no longer serves us. Through this doorway access to the eternal light is opened. Fire converts matter into energy and through this energy we can transform.

Air

This is the breath of life, our movement and our flow. It swiftly takes us to other places. From the connection with air, we can communicate simultaneously on all levels. Air helps us to expand ourselves in all directions, thus helping the soul to fully express itself. The element of air allows us to feel less restricted and helps us to expand more in all directions. It therefore helps us to maximise our soul potential.

Earth

Earth connects the soul to its planetary grounding, providing stability to the connection the soul needs at a particular time. It is the stable energy that feeds us. The earth helps to provide structure and holds the balance of everything. Earth seeks to ensure that everything is secure, it provides a safe container.

Water

Water holds the cellular memory of the earth. Water seeks to enable us to go deep within our souls, connecting us to who we are at a soul level and connecting us with our own cellular memory. From connecting with water, we are able to connect to hidden depths of ourselves.

Angels

Angels are high frequency beings connected to the energy of love. This is an energy form that is available to the healer, if it is an energy that they are already connected to. This opens the doors to the frequencies of love. Angels express through the frequencies of love, and it is the energy that brings in compassion to the altar. Love and compassion connect our hearts together into oneness and enable the healer to work compassionately with love.

Stars

Scientists state that all humans are connected to the stars. It is also the case that many of our ancestors are from the stars. Stars can also help to connect to ancestral origins, as the stars have always aided humanity to navigate in different aspects of the universe. Some souls have a stronger connection with the stars. Many souls have spent lifetimes on the evolved stars, such as Orion and Sirius B, for their learning and to help the earth with its evolution. Calling in this energy opens the connection to the stars of those connected to this, and the energy helps brings in qualities of galactic and ancient wisdom that is here to help Earth evolution.

Dragons

The dragon energy brings a powerful protective energy into the space. The dragon energy is a warrior energy that empowers all who connect with this. Some healers have a strong connection with this energy and see the dragons when they call this energy into their altar. Dragons were involved in the creation of the earth. They also act as protectors in all aspects of time.

The Energetic Hut

The energetic hut helps to provide a structure for an ancestral healing session. There is the gifted traditional healer who can channel advice from the ancestors and there is the rare traditional healer who can manifest the voices of the ancestors for clients to hear. In the African Zulu tradition, the spirits whistling inside a hut, is described by the author Barbara Tyrrell, to be "speech of the old ones". It is a profound gift to witness. In some traditions in Africa, the medicine man or woman will see their clients in a wooden hut. This creates a sacred space where divination and healing can take place. It also provides a protective space away from preying eyes and other energies that may try to interfere in the process.

To empower ancestral healers with their healing practice I initiated them into the energetic hut. This is used and manifested for themselves and their clients. This is invoked energetically by the mind. This is an alchemical process that provides an energetic space of protection and structure, within which healing work can take place. The ancestral practitioner sits opposite the client; he or she requests the gatekeeper on the father's line to step forward to the right of the client and the gatekeeper on the mother's line to step forward on the left side. The reason why ancestors on both sides are invoked, is because it provides the opportunity for both ancestral fields to be present. The ancestral gatekeeper, who is connected to the problem that the client is facing, will step forward and will convey the information to help with the origin of the problem. An important part of ancestral work is a strong mind; a strong spirit; and strong protection.

The energetic hut provides a safe space to invoke the gatekeepers of the client to step forward, after the altar has been opened. The gatekeepers are ancestors of a particular frequency who have agreed to step forward so that divination can take place with the healer and the ancestor. Gatekeepers are messengers on behalf of the ancestors, the spokesperson, the caregivers and the receivers. They are a vessel for information, which automatically transmits down the ancestral line from the thousands of ancestors. The gatekeeper also acts as a spokesperson for those ancestors who may be stuck in their own shadow, or from their movement on their path that is affecting the client. The healing work is focused on the client healing of ancestral patterns which need to be healed, connected to an ancestor or ancestral collective issue. The receptors of the gatekeeper feed the information that provides a lightning flash to what is needed, to liberate the individual from unhealthy patterns. The healer receives this information and uses their energetic toolkit, to complete the healing process and to liberate the energy that is needed from the client and affected ancestors.

After the invocation of the gatekeepers, the tool of power will be invoked between the client and the healer. The energetic hut allows an experience that is not detrimental to either party. This energetic hut acts as a container for those involved in this work. It also provides concealment and invisibility to other forces that may try to stop this work; it provides a secure place. Engaging in an ancestral field is only for students who have been initiated or trained because this field is full of distortion, often from thousands of years of trauma and dissociation from its origin. This requires a strong structure with strong boundaries and protection. Structure and process is an important part of ancestral work; as are a strong mind; a strong spirit; and strong protection.

Divination

I connected with the word divination when connecting with the ancestral method that I developed; it felt an appropriate word rather than using the word channelling. Divination is a method of discovering what is unknown; what is concealed; or hidden. It is the key practice in ancestral healing work because discovering the origin of the problem is the key to resolving an ancestral issue. There are many different divination techniques that are completed by indigenous healers. As described by the author John Janzev in his book, *Ngoma*, Swazi divinership in Africa is: "A healing ritual called ukuvumisa when the Sangoma is possessed by the ancestors". After this possession the Sangoma completes divination for their clients. He also describes that the Tangoma tribe use a divination technique of throwing bones. It is said that the ancestral spirits influence how the bones fall and the patterns this creates. The diviner completes their diagnosis based on the patterns that are created and which they have learnt to interpret to pass on the guidance from the ancestors.

To complete ancestral healing the healer needs to have strong divination skills, to track the origin of what is causing the problem in the ancestral field and heal this at its core. It is a method that enables awareness of the different fields that exist in the ancestral field. This enables the healer to see into the hearts of the client, which is the gateway of the soul. It also enables the healer to convey the ancestral stories that have been forgotten or are not known about. The loss of the oral transmission of ancestral stories in many cultures can contribute to humanity forgetting their ancestral past and the reasons for suffering. Divination helps to understand our relationships with our ancestors and the reasons for distortion in our ancestral fields. It also helps to discover how we fit into the ancestral web and connects us with ancestors and ancestral stories that we were not aware of.

I was guided to develop a divination technique using cowrie shells. There are many cultures that use cowrie shells as part of their divination practice. Many African countries along with many Afro-American regions use cowrie shells for divination. The number of shells used can vary from 4 – 16 divination shells to complete readings. For example, the Obi tradition use four cowrie shells and the top of the cowrie shells are cut off. This form of divination gives Yes or No answers. The diviner will ask what the client needs help with. The throwing of the divination shells will only give a Yes or No answer. They are thrown and depending on the combination which shows itself, an answer will be given.

For the divination method that I developed I use 10 cowrie shells. Cowrie shells are from water; water holds cellular memory of the earth and these shells are great tools to activate this in ancestral divination work. The shells are also connected to femininity. Our mother birthed us into this world with all the memory we hold, so it is powerful that the shells are connected to this energy. The more the diviner works with these shells, the greater the accuracy of information that is given. The number one is connected to the physical, so it is apt that the number of cowrie shells used should start with this number. Ten is also the number of love and light, throwing these cowrie shells paves the way to illuminate that which is hidden and that which is ready to be seen. Ten is also a symbol of wholeness. The number ten also has the energies contained within this of the masculine and feminine. Navigating our ancestral fields of course starts with these energies, which give birth to our reality. From the number 10 life is manifested one is life in the physical and the zero symbolises our return to our soul, our source aspect.

Before the divination stage takes place, healers will have already used their altar to call in their protectors, invoked their energetic hut and invoked their tool of power.

To complete the divination, they follow the following steps:

1. Ask your client what they need help with.
2. Hold the shells in your hands with the intention of finding out the information to help and connect to the spiritual teacher.
3. Place your hand 10 inches above the divination board.
4. Drop the shells over your divination board.
5. Tune into the board and let the ancestral field talk to the ancestral healer, with the answers, paying attention to where the shells fall, near to the areas on the divination board.

Please note; only use this divination board if you have been initiated into ancestral energetic work by a spiritual teacher. The divination board is what I channelled and developed. The divination board is not pictured in this book as an initiation into this is required, to use this safely and effectively.

Ancestral Story
Soul release

There are extraordinary stories that come out of divination practice. I recall in my own healing practice helping Dean who was suffering from depression. After divination, it was found that this was linked to his energetic connection to his grandfather. His father was a soldier in World War One. There was an aspect of his grandfather's soul, which was stuck in the trauma of the war and this was affecting his health. I connected to the energy of his grandfather at that time and sent in energy to release the aspect of his grandfather's soul who was stuck there. As I completed this release, his grandfather also released with him his comrades who had been trapped in the same aspect of time. This divination and healing ritual healed the client, released his grandfather's soul trapped in the trauma of war and healed a collective of souls who were also freed from being stuck in the same aspect of time. Ancestral healing really does have an important impact on the collective; it is important work for the earth.

Elements Connection Exercise

This is an exercise to help you to connect safely and easily with the elements, air, earth, water and fire. Find a comfortable place to sit in nature. Have 4 stones with you. Put these stones in front of you. Place one stone which represents air, in the energetic north. Place another stone to represent the energetic east, this will represent the fire. Place another in south for earth, and finally place a stone in the energetic west to represent the water.

Start with air and call in the element of air to be with you in your mind. You can imagine you are connecting to the wind, as you do connect to the qualities that air has to offer.

Connect to the element of fire in the east, and call in the qualities that this has to offer you. As you do, you can imagine that you are connecting to the sun.

Connect to the element of earth in the south. Connect to the earth on the ground where you are sitting and connect to the qualities it has to offer.

Connect to the element of water. As you do you can imagine you are connecting to the rain or the waters of rivers or lakes and connect to the qualities that these have to offer.

Do this ritual regularly to connect to the consciousness of the elements to help you connect more with nature and to be in harmony with it. It will also help you to be in more harmony with yourself. It is a very powerful healing process.

Ancestral Wisdom

Navigating the ancestral fields is the initiation into compassionate warriorship, for within these fields are light and dark energies. Sometimes the dark aspects of the shadow can be challenging and confrontational. In many ways, this is to be expected as ancestral work helps to connect to great wisdom that is contained within the shadow aspects and often hidden. This can create great healing not only for one person but also a collective. It can be expected that sometimes this will be fiercely guarded, depending on the types of energies that are connected with the ancestral lineage, or spirits may try to stop the connection.

Traditional healers and healers in indigenous cultures have paved the way for the great wisdom that we have today to help those in need. There is proof that many people have been healed by healers connected to strong energetic practices, that have often produced miraculous healings. They are taught these processes by their elders and their spirits. In the same way that I was taught these practices, to help create ancestral healers to complete powerful practices, who are aligned to the evolutionary energies of now.

This chapter has outlined the fundamentals of safe practice when completing ancestral healing work. These processes should only be completed by healers who have been safely initiated into these processes by a teacher. This includes; connecting with a spiritual teacher, a specialist in ancestral work; calling in their protectors via a magical altar; invoking an energetic hut; and calling in tools of power. This provides a safe space to complete divination and to find the origin of the problem. With all shamanic practices, the alignment with the spiritual teams is the key to powerful work. Working regularly with these energetic practices and your spiritual teams, creates a magical practice and healings for the clients. Navigating the ancestral fields effectively helps pinpoint the origin of the problem to implement profound healing. Pinpointing and healing the origin of an ancestral problem could also have an effect of changing the DNA distortion in the ancestral field forever.

Ancestral healing is extremely rewarding work and these healers are called to do this work by their spirits, in the same way that I was called to do so. Ancestral healers who work in this field often go to another level of their spiritual self because they are initiated into being more empowered at a soul level. Specialist guides step forward to help them, along with their own ancestors who stand proudly celebrating the work they are doing to help humanity.

Chapter 3

Curses: Distorting Ancestral Reality

*The wrath of man inflicts on its own misery and
pain that can continue down the generations.*

What Are Curses?

Curses are powerful energies, which create powerful distortions in
the ancestral fields. They distort two fields; firstly, from the curser
or the person who has arranged the curse and secondly, the distortion
it causes to the victim or group of soul's energetic fields. Any action
that is not aligned with our source origin creates fragmentation. A
curse is from the Anglo-Saxon word cursian meaning 'to invoke harm
or evil upon'. A curse is a malediction, spoken or written to make
the malefactor suffer or die, or to prophesy harm to evildoers. The
infliction of curses on other people does exist, as does the ability to
afflict these on other people. Curses create distortions in time within
the affected ancestral field, because the disturbed field disrupts the
natural flow of the soul or collective of souls affected. This manifests
a disturbance, which creates particular behaviour or illness to reflect
what has happened. However, this can be reconfigured to help the soul
continue their journey to wholeness. Curses act as antennae to help
anchor those qualities that they have created into the consciousness

of humanity. Some of humanity feed into this energy and have learnt rituals to gain power over other people and so the behaviour it creates continues.

Our connection to our ancestral fields shows the story of the disharmony that humanity has created, creating separation from each other. The implementation of curses magnifies humanity's worse attributes, while inflicting a huge energy on an individual or a collective that can hinder an aspect of a soul journey. The energy that drives other people to inflict curses is one of individualism and abuse of power. This creates separation between people. This also creates a consciousness in the collective, which is connected to the individual needs of humanity. As the author Max Gluckman in his book, *Custom and Conflict in Africa* describes; "The witch wants to hurt people he hates, has quarrelled with, of whom he is envious".

It is often for individual gain that energetic power in the form of curses is used to inflict control on other people. When a curse is implemented, a distortion is created from our source aspect. We can say that humanity steps into their own darkness and shadow. To evolve and grow, our shadow aspect and our source light are playing together like a cosmic song to sing us back home into the pure manifestation of being. We have free will so we can heal our shadow and work through this for our evolution, or we can inflict harm on others for our own personal gain.

Factors Driving Humanity to Curse Other People

The curser who is employed, or who inflicts the will of his or her own intentions on other people, is driven by a number of key factors.

Greed: this can be connected to payment being received for the implementation of curses, or the desire to have more ownership or money. Greed is an emotion that drives an ambition of attainment. It is normally reflected by what society has created of materialism, and what is of value and perceived status.

Envy: envy shows its energy in many ways. Envy produces the need to sabotage and change what another person has. The energy of envy can overwhelm the person who is experiencing this and create an emotional charge to inflict pain on other people.

Power: the need to be the more powerful over another person, or to prove how powerful a person is. Power games between individuals and societies permeate strongly. There is sometimes the drive to reduce someone's power, or show how powerful you are by creating controlling behaviour, which creates psychological bondage. For example, a community knowing that a magician has the ability to implement curses, may begin to live in psychological fear of this person, giving the magician status and power.

Manipulation: implementing curses can be a way to manipulate another person for personal gain. Curses can create thought forms to the victim so they can be manipulated into a way of behaviour that is not aligned with their soul, turning a person into a zombie type state that is easily manipulated by other people. The energy of curses can sometimes have entities attached and these can feed in negative thought forms to the victims.

Control: curses can be inflicted to disempower other people and therefore make it easier to control the behaviour of the victim. There is strong psychology attached to the belief of receiving a curse. As a consequence, it may become easier for the perpetrator of the curse to control the person who has received this.

Possession: a curse can be implemented to take possession of a person, or completely take their mind so they cannot think clearly for themselves, constantly living in a victim like state of being. Curses like these could be used to obtain the affections of someone, or to control someone into a way of thinking. The person who has implemented a curse, also causes a distortion in their own field, which goes down the ancestral generations. This will play out in various ways, until the soul works through the karmic patterns that have been created.

Ancestral Story
Depression

An ancestral healer worked with Becky who normally had a positive attitude and happy demeanour. She started a new job and subsequently lost a lot of confidence, self-esteem and developed depression and intense anxiety. Becky was unable to sleep properly, waking up suddenly with a jerk, and she had a continual sinking feeling in the stomach and in her solar plexus area. Through divination, it was found that her colleagues in the new team were connected in a past life. In particular, one team member who she was having problems with, Becky had put a curse on this team member in a past life. Through the divination, she saw that Becky in the past life was a man, who was married to his now colleague. In the past lifetime the client had three children, and the children are also part of the work team in this current life. In the past life, Becky discovered that his partner was working for both the light and dark. He wanted to protect the children from being manipulated by their auntie who was working with dark energy. He was fearful of her children practising work of the dark and was very protective over them. He did not want the aunt in the children's life, and to protect his children, cast a curse on the aunt to bind her from practising any 'magic or light or dark work' at all. The energy of this past life reappeared to be working out in this lifetime. The aunt from the past life now reappeared in Becky's life as a work colleague, and she constantly threw 'psychological daggers' at her in the current life psychically attacking the client, and causing her to feel depressed and unable to function effectively in the team.

The ancestral healer asked Becky if she was willing to undo the curse and also send forgiveness to both herself and her work colleague. The past life version of herself was asked to be present for the healing. She said a forgiveness statement and asked for the curse to be undone. Rattling was performed around her and during this the daggers were removed from the back of Becky, who suffered from back pain. To further perform healing and cleansing, she swam and dunked herself in the sea as this healing ritual was performed outside on the beach. Becky's feedback was that she felt a lot more grounded, confident and the anxiety had gone since the healing. She felt back to her normal self and was able to be more assertive and take control within the team. Healing had taken place to heal the distortion in her energetic field created by the energy of inflicting a curse on other people; she had healed the ancestral self.

The Impact of Curses

The impact of curses on the ancestral field is related to a dysfunctional approach to love and harmony. Curses have created a malfunction in the quantum field, which created an opening for manifestations of thoughts that were not in alignment with source. This created the need to inflict power and control on other people and thus the infliction of curses was one of these ways. Curses are a means of controlling society into a particular way of being, behaviour, and creating a power hierarchy of being. From implementing curses, an aspect of self can manifest in the form of demons. These are manifestations of energies that are so wrapped up with guilt, negative thought forms or pure darkness. This aspect of self can remain in a whirlwind of energy, until the appropriate time when the energies can move out of this. They can manifest at the time when the person who implemented the curse, plays out in an aspect of the soul at some stage of the soul journey. As described by the author Alfred Ribi, in his book *Demons of The Inner World:* "Elements in the collective unconscious (archetypes) transform into evil demons, when they are no longer worshiped and represented in consciousness".

Harmonising curses and the removal of the need of humanity to inflict curses, is one of the keys to evolution. While this is at play, cycles continue to be created that create pain for other people. It fragments from the source-self, community and nature. Survival mode and desperation can sometimes create desperate acts. Arguments about lovers, land, jealously and who is the most powerful can create and can lead someone to connect to a sorcerer for a quick fix to a problem. These negative impulses of humanity need to be harmonised in the collective and ancestral healing is one important way that can create a huge impact. There are many healers who heal curses by going into energetic battles with the perpetrators of the curses in past or present life, or by making deals with the perpetrators who inflicted the curses. None of this is required to effectively harmonise and release a curse. What is needed is to have a strong gift of divination, strong connection with your spiritual teams, and working from the heart with strong protection and working from love and compassion.

Curses are created to gain power over other people, and can switch and change according to the frequency of who they are connected to. The aim of a curse is to inflict control and to manipulate other people. The impact of curses is that they create negative thought forms; these can be of fear, victim, loss of control, and loss of power. Curses and the perpetrators who inflict them are acting in a way of keeping consciousness in thought forms that take humanity away from the source energy of love. It is a very powerful energetic force that has been having a hold on consciousness and the ancestral fields for a long time. It is inevitable that ancestors will be affected by a curse that has been placed on an ancestor or collective of ancestors.

Thought forms created by curses can include any or more of the following feelings:

- powerlessness
- fear
- low self-esteem
- ancestral illness
- fragmentation from the source

Curses cause intrusions in the energy field which affects the vibration of the energy field. The energy can also attach to particular parts of the body, such as around the solar plexus, and create illness, as they create stuck energy and feed in negative energy. There is no doubt that this also creates a distortion in the DNA. Epigenetics discusses how DNA is influenced by the environment. There are many symptoms of curses, which are discussed later in this chapter. These intrusions have an effect on the individual and down the ancestral line. They cause a change in vibrational frequency and connect the field to energetic thought forms connected to the curse that plays out in the physical reality. Our thoughts create our reality and so it is also the case of thought forms connected to curses playing out in our energetic fields. It also creates a connection between the person who has been cursed and the person who cursed them.

The implementation of curses causes a distortion in the energy field, which can lead to other energies further attaching themselves to the victim, such as entities. This causes further disharmony in the energy field, which causes a ripple effect in the ancestral field. Curses create traits that are passed down the generations silently, until the reason for the origin of a problem is revealed and harmonised by a healer, skilled in this area of work, or this is worked off karmically. The pain of being the victim of a curse or the perpetrator, can lead the person to help other people with similar issues. In this time of earth evolution an ancestral healer releasing a curse can lead to thousands of souls attached to the ancestral line affected by this, being liberated from this field of existence that may have played out in their energy field for thousands of years. This in turn allows aspects of the soul to continue their journey. It also helps to heal the collective shadow of the planet and therefore contribute to planetary evolution.

Humanity has created many malignant fields of existence to take humanity away from their divine connection with nature and the source. In the divine source creation, we are whole and in harmony. The fragmented state caused by the impact of a curse, creates an alternate field where fear can manifest and grow. Curses can often be arranged by close family members on other family members, creating a karmic cycle, which is passed through the generations. These soul members meet time and time again during various incarnations to heal what has been done before.

Those perpetrators who create curses can sometimes be masters in creating a thought form of fear to their victims. Many can be master psychologists, without implementing a genuine curse, but letting their victims feel that they have done so. There are people who are able to inflict powerful curses on other people, and although there is a small minority who have this ability, they can work in a very powerful way. Curses that were implemented in past lives tend to be very powerful. The evolution of man unfolds over time, revealing the victim or the perpetrator and will reveal itself in the appropriate lifetime, when the soul is ready to evolve to the appropriate level of its evolution. The energy of curses will always play out in the psyche and will manifest itself in the appropriate way, when the time presents itself for this to be part of the soul journey.

I worked with a client who was having terrible dreams of being attacked by demonic forces and she felt the presence of demons in her home. The story unfolded that she had been a witch in a past life and had inflicted a terrible curse on many people. This demonic aspect of herself was playing out in the present time reality and coming up for healing. She healed this aspect by asking forgiveness from the collective she affected and also forgave herself. The torment she was experiencing dissipated and she was able to sleep properly again. Everything that is in our unconscious and psyche can be projected; only by delving into what is being projected will we reveal the true story around what is playing out in a person's ancestral field of existence.

Curses and the implementation of curses are embedded in some cultures and are part of daily life. The author Edward Evans-Pritchard in his book *Witchcraft, Oracles and Magic Amongst the Azande*, describes that in the Azande tradition witchcraft is seen as a psychic act, whereas a sorcerer can potentially cause harm by performing; "magic rites with bad medicine". This bad medicine as he describes, creates a collective field in the consciousness of a society, which is bound into a certain way of being. This is based on fields of energy connected to control, fear and manipulation. Those who are constantly exposed to such emotions in their culture will have these energies playing out in their energetic fields, which are passed down the generations.

Ancestral Story
Fear of stepping into one's own power

An ancestral healer worked with Mary who from a young age had mental health problems. These included suicidal thoughts and she felt restricted about stepping into her own power. She also felt very restricted by her mother. Tracking the origin of the problem via divination, the healer found that it related to a past life when Mary was a member of a round table. It was revealed that many of these members were distinguished as light workers, but they were in fact working with dark energy. They taught the rest of the members to complete an energetic act and tricked them into thinking it was good, when in fact it had bad consequences. As a result, a curse was put on the group by someone outside the group, to prevent them practising again. As a consequence of this curse there were also entities attached to the entire group, along with a powerful sorceress entity. To release this energy, a forgiveness statement was made to all the collective of souls who were involved at this time. Entities were also removed that were connected to the energy of this time and from those involved in the dark acts. Follow-up work given to Mary included working on forgiveness of those people who had bullied Mary as a child and also forgiveness towards her mother, whom she had never felt accepted by. This work freed Mary from this energy and thus her future generations.

Types of Curses

There are many different types of curses, some of which are described below.

Celtic: the evil eye; a prolonged stare causing misfortune. This is a case of highly concentrated will power aimed solely at the person or object involved. These hold their roots in mythology, folk magic, and charms.

Magicians and Shamans: the world shaman comes from the Siberian Evenk and Manchu word Saman or Samman and means either to know, or to become heated. The shamans help the community with healing and divination and so on. They are at one with the spirits they work with, which work through them when they are working. Many shamans work for the good of their community. However, there are some shamans and healers that have powerful powers to put curses on other people.

The word magician is a person with magical powers. Both the magician and the shaman often work for the good to help other people. However, there are some who can work to inflict curses and misery on other people. These are powerful, due to the ability of the magician and shaman to work in a powerful way with energy.

The author Bruce Kapferrer in his book, *The Feast of the Sorcerer,* discusses how: "Sorcery does not conceive of human beings as isolates but as engaged in a web of affective ties or relations". Ritualistic curses are some of the most powerful curses. The magician will use the relationship between nature and unseen forces to cause harm to other human beings. This can involve the use of animal and human sacrifices. An element such as fire and air may also be used. Some shamans use chant and ecstatic dance to move into a state of full spirit possession to inflict curses on their enemies. When inflicting a curse, the magician may request for an element and a demonic spirit to inflict misery or an illness on another person, and send this as an energy force to them. When someone is aligned powerfully with spirits, this is inflicted easily onto another person.

Objects such as dolls and puppets can also be used as part of the process of creating curses. A symbol is given to the object, for example relating to the person to whom the curse is directed and this can also be dressed like the person. The perpetrator of the curse will treat the object how he or she wishes the person to be treated. This curse is sent energetically to the person on whom the curse is to be inflicted. When removing curses, the energy also has to be removed from the object that has been used as part of the curse.

Egyptian Curses: during ancient Egyptian times some of the strongest curses were implemented, and often placed on the dead. These curses used concentrated thoughts and words and inscriptions on tombs. The author Stuart Gordon in his book, *The Book of Curses,* describes that the French Egyptologist Mardrus stated: "I am absolutely convinced that ancient Egyptians knew how to concentrate upon and around a mummy using certain dynamic powers." The most famous curses were those that were attached to tombs. In ancient Egyptian times, curses were sometimes placed at the entrances of tombs to protect the tombs, mummies and the journey of the spirits of the deceased into the afterlife. Sometimes the energy of the curse was inscribed in the tomb chamber, on the walls and on other areas. Most of the Egyptian curses were metaphysical. However, sometimes booby traps and poison was used.

Egyptian spells were powerful to protect and powerful to cause misfortune and misery to other people. Spell casting was defined by the word Heka. Words were pronounced in certain ways to deliver certain power and spells of protection and spells against other people. There was a language of sound with the words that linked a magical force to the present. Wax figures were also used as part of spell rituals and these were crushed, or spat at, and burned to complete a ritual of spell casting.

Religious or God Curses: curses by gods and religion had a detrimental effect on other people, for example Adam and Eve being expelled from the Garden of Eden. Early on in history, factors of religious orders were involved in curses to maintain control. There are many mythological stories of gods inflicting curses on other people.

Jinx or Hex: this type of curse may refer to such a wish or pronouncement, which is made effective by a supernatural or spiritual power. This can include a god or gods, a spirit or a natural force, or else as a kind of spell by magic or witchcraft, which is directed to a person. With this type of curse objects can be deliberately charged with fatal energy. Objects are used to represent the person and the negative energy placed in this. Jinxes are different from curses in that ill luck is not caused by malign or deliberate intent, but sometimes by fatal accident or mischance. This causes a death or agony so intense that this creates an imprint on objects connected with the disaster, along with an imprint within the soul of the person who has been affected. It is important when releasing curses, that the energy of a curse is also taken out of an object.

Generational Curses: these are particular curses which are implemented to affect generations down a particular ancestral lineage. Cursing a family and their forefathers has been a common curse that has been implemented over many generations. They are powerful because they directly affect those people who are connected to an ancestral lineage and impact the genes of those people affected and are a contributory cause to a genetic propensity to a particular illness and behaviour.

These could be:

- an evil spell attached to a person ration of genes
- the implementation of an energy and power to inflict evil on a person or group ancestral line which are connected by genes
- a curse that causes misery or death attached to a person's ancestral lineage
- a demonic phenomenon that transports demons and demonic tendencies to the second ancestral generation. This demonic presence may be attached to the curse that has been placed on a family.

Symptoms of a Curse

The symptoms listed do not always mean that someone definitely has a curse attached to them, but these symptoms can be connected to a person who has a curse on them. Curses, as previously discussed, cause distortions in the energy fields and therefore can create a number of different physical and emotional problems:

- a repeated, similar chronic illness down the ancestral line
- mental and or emotional breakdowns
- marital breakdown or family alienation
- persistent financial insufficiency
- being accident prone
- a history of suicides, unnatural or untimely deaths.

Ancestral Story
Mental illness

Tony suffered from mental illness and depression for most of his life, but had no present life trauma. When divination was completed it was found that there was an entity attached to a curse, which had been attached to the family for generations. The story behind the curse was that a member of the family had a curse placed on them, as a result of a dispute over land. A landowner was jealous of the land that his ancestors had and arranged for a curse to be placed on his family. This curse carried with it the feeling of disempowerment, sadness and fear, which continued down the generations. Energetic work was completed to release the curse and entity. After the session, the client felt lighter and more able to continue their life. This had not only freed the client, but also had freed this energy from his ancestral lineage.

Tracking and Healing Curses

Protectors and Guides

To heal and release a curse training is needed by a respected spiritual teacher, as curses are very powerful dark energies. The aim of the ancestral healer is to break the link between the person who implemented the curse and the victim of the curse. Also, to release the curse from the energetic field of all those people who are affected by it.

To release curses there needs to be a strong connection to spiritual guides. When I train students to be ancestral practitioners, I help them to connect to a number of guides, including guides which specialise in removing curses. There are many powerful guides working for the highest good. One ancestral practitioner connected to her guide to help with curse release, this was a huge green dragon. The dragon works by pulling out the curse from the object and person affected. The dragon transmutes the curse by breathing fire on it. The dragon also alerts the ancestral healer practitioner to the presence of the existence of the curse through a feeling of tiredness, which the practitioner feels in their energetic field, along with communicating wisdom on this.

Another guide which showed up for a healer was a Chinese sage, with a heart as large as the sun. The sun is used to purify and send love. When she worked with her first case for curses, both of her guides turned up, and the Chinese sage rode on the back of the dragon to combine both powers to help. The curse guide dealt with the curse by purification, filling the client with love and sending love to the perpetrator too and the dragon gave strength and protection.

Tracking the Curse

To deal effectively with and heal a curse, the healer needs to have a strong connection to their spiritual teams and the practitioner needs to track the cycle of the curse. Divination and working with the spiritual guides using the process below helps to achieve this. As already stated, this work can only be completed if the practitioner has been initiated and trained to complete this process by a teacher competent in this area of work, and should not be completed by anyone who has not been trained.

1. Know the story
   • What is the story in the ancestral lineage?
   • Where did the origin of the curse come from?

There are many stories that can form the background behind a curse. This could be a spurred lover or a dispute over land. It is important that through divination the story of the curse is known, so the ancestral healer can become aware of all participants who are involved in the curse and complete the necessary work to heal and transform.

2. A person or a collective
   - Who is it that instigated the curse?
   - Is it an individual or collective?

Who is the person who instigated the curse, or was it a group? All parties involved in this need to be part of the process to effectively release a curse. For example, you may have a mother-in-law who went to a magician to put a curse on her daughter-in-law. So, both the magician and the daughter-in-law are involved in implementing the curse.

3. Identify the attacker or magician
   - Who implemented the curse?

Who is the person who sent the curse to the victim? This needs to be identified in the energetic field.

4. Identify the thought form associated with the curse
   - Fear? Victim? Manipulation and so on?

What thought forms were created in the curse when it was sent? This is important because thought forms have energy and these need to be healed, so the energy can be taken out to free the victim of the curse.

A thought form connected with a curse is a thought form that is artificially created via a magical energy. This is given a form and a shape and within this thought form a purpose is created. It may be for protection or in the form of a spell or aggression towards another person. To create these requires a lot of energy and precise programming. As with all curses, thought forms that were created in ancient times can be extremely powerful.

5. Type of energy associated with the curse
   - Dark, difficult?

The healer needs to know the energy they are dealing with. Is it easy or very difficult energy to deal with? This requires the appropriate preparation when preparing to release this energy.

6. What is the element attached to this?
   * Fire, water?

There is often an element that is sent with a curse, it is useful to track what this is. Elements are living consciousness, so harmonising the element involved is important.

7. Track the sound associated with the curse

Everything omits sound. Some practitioners are gifted in being able to track a curse via its energetic sound. This enables a way of locating the energy of the curse.

8. Is there an object associated with the curse?
   * What does this look like?

Dolls or objects created to represent a person are sometimes used to implement curses. Sometimes these may have cloth or hair belonging to the person they are attached to them. Sometimes pins are placed in the body to cause illness, bringing in destructive energy.

9. Any psychology involved?

Is there any psychology involved by the magician to the victim? For example, instilling fear that needs to be harmonised in the energetic field.

Self-Awareness Exercise

Take these steps to help transform any large emotional negative energy you may have directed towards someone in your life.

1. Write down a time when you may have directed negative energy towards a person, when you were upset in this present life.
2. Write down the situation that caused this and the emotions you felt.
3. Make a list of the negative thought forms you felt towards this person.
4. For each negative thought form, create a direct positive one.
5. Arrange a ceremony for yourself in nature or at home.
6. Connect to your heart and allow all these negative thoughts and emotions towards the person to be released from your energy body and allow the earth to take this beneath your feet.
7. Connect to your heart and allow these positive thoughts to be sent to this person unconditionally.

Ancestral Wisdom

Humanity's move to abuse of power and wanting to be in control of other people has created the implementation of curses in the first place. When members of humanity become more in harmony with each other the driving force behind the need to implement curses will be removed. Survival has often been associated with the need to be ahead of other people, when in fact when we remove this energy thought form, there is a realisation that there is enough for everyone. The implementation of curses, not only affects those people who receive this but also their ancestors. It also affects the person who implemented this and their ancestral lineage.

Curses are the most powerful forces affecting humanity. They are not easy to deal with and only can be healed by healers who are trained in this area. Another win-win situation is a mass rise in consciousness on the earth and more people working from the heart and with love. This is forming a powerful ripple affect that can really shine light to these areas, and can engineer change.

Curses are one of the most powerful ways of distorting the energetic fields of those people who are affected. Healing curses from the individual and the collective is very important. Curses in the ancestral energetic fields are creating illness and behaviour that is repeating down the generations. We have much to learn from the stories behind curses and how this links to the disharmony that exists within humanity. Curses are real and powerful they have created distortion in the human energy field and DNA down the ancestral lines, being free of these distortions helps future generations.

Reflection time

*Write your insights, healing and tasks moving
forward to continue to heal your life.*

Chapter 4

Entities: Manifestation of the Shadows

There is a tunnel of consciousness that illuminates all that is hidden, setting free the entrapments of your soul.

What is an Entity?

An entity is a spirit, which has no body. Entities come in many different forms and show themselves in many different ways. The entities I perceive to be connected with the distortion in the ancestral fields are described here. Freeing the soul of such aspects of ancestral distortions, which entities are part of, and other circumstances, is the key to soul and planetary evolution. An entity can be described as a container of knowledge in the realms of spirit, particularly for the individual and the collective.

Entities are part of our existence, and denying them is denying aspects of ourselves that exist in the universe; they are connected to us all. To reject them is to limit the possibilities of wisdom that we can evolve through. They can show us aspects of our shadow, which we often deny to ourselves. We need to allow observations of this when it is appropriate. Not all entities are aspects of our shadow, but it is good to be aware that at times they can be.

When we hear the word entity it can instil fear. Behind every entity is a story and the story can be to do with the woes of humanity. This is the case particularly within the ancestral fields. This story can be one of inflicted will on other people, connected to factors such as abuse of power, and instilling fear in other people. This can create trauma, and consequently someone could have an entity attachment. It is easy to be in fear of such forms, maybe because of religious backgrounds or from what has been written in books. Most entities have been light source beings at some stage; many have lost their connection to the light. Some may have been souls who had suffered great trauma and were disconnected from source, by entering into an entity existence. Some entities are easier to deal with than others and healers should always protect themselves when completing entity release work.

Entities can be spokespersons for the collective shadow. Their work is often to deflate the expansion of the soul. When they attach to other people, they wish to influence behaviour in the direction of their own thought forms. They are way-showers that create a web of consciousness that at times can create dysfunctional behaviour. At the forefront of their existence can be dogma from the higher hierarchy of the shadow with no negotiation, which keeps many entities trapped and existing in a motionless existence.

The connection between an entity and a person can occur in various ways. It can occur due to the person having some vulnerability in their energy field. This is the spiritual energy field that surrounds the human form. Vulnerability in the energy field can be related to extensive trauma, for example: past life karmic issues; anger; depression; addiction; and not protecting the energy field when completing spiritual work. It could also be due to delving into dark magic, or a past life where there was an abuse of power, which caused harm to other people. Vulnerability in the energy field creates a disturbance in the energy field, which makes this less whole and fragmented. The effect of this ripples down the ancestral line and manifests in various forms, which can include addictive behaviour and ancestral illness.

Roles of Entities

How energy became an entity or the origins of an entity is a worthy area to explore, as this raises our awareness of the fact that nothing is separate, they are also our ancestors. The connection between entities and ancestral healing is related in many cases to fragmentation of the soul created by trauma. Many entities are fragmented from the divine light of their being. By their nature they can operate and manifest in different realities. Like any energetic being, they are attracted to those energies with similar frequencies and sounds, or who have vulnerability in their energetic fields. This is what they know in their own perceived reality. Entities can be earth-bound spirits who have been incarnated on Earth, but for a variety of reasons after they have died, they have remained on the earth plane. This can have an impact on the energetic fields of the affected ancestor, because this is a stuck energy of an ancestral soul who has not moved forward and this has a rippling effect on the ancestral field.

Some entities can remember their time on Earth or other planes of existence and to some extent their source light. Other entities are so wrapped up in guilt or negativity that they have no remembrance of life in any other form, or of access to the higher frequencies of the source light. Such entities remain in an emotionless existence, constantly wrapped in a field of negativity and fear of moving on and they are constantly fuelled by fields of negativity of thought forms and sounds. These can be created by their own thought forms, or from negative thought forms sent to them by other entities to keep them in their darkness.

All entities leave their imprint in consciousness in the same way that all energetic beings do. Such an imprint in consciousness is useful because it allows for the ancestral story relating to entities to be accessed and healed. Entities that are not aligned with love, have contributed to distortions in the DNA, because their attachments or negative behaviour causes a distortion in a person's energy field. The result is the creation of similar characteristics down the ancestral lines, such as alcoholism, mental health and illness, which continue down the generations. Entities are archetypal energies of what humanity has created by cursing, fear, control, manipulation and abuse of power. Entities are therefore in the mind of the qualities which have been created, and many cannot move out of these revolving thoughts and energy. Such energy creates a further pull away from the light.

Entities are attracted to people who are into power, but not for the highest good. If they are able, they will penetrate their energetic fields and work on influencing thoughts and behaviour, often in a negative way. If the person is in a position of great power, the impact on a collective can be devastating. Some souls have also made a karmic choice to work with these energies. Attracting entities is also about our thoughts, lifestyle and what we choose to bring into our lives. If our ancestors have abused their power and have adversely affected a collective, this also affects the ancestral field and ancestral healing work needs to take place to heal this field of energy.

We can look at the collective trauma of slavery in any culture. This has many individuals and groups of souls trapped by this trauma and this affects the ancestral field. Releasing one soul from this also simultaneously allows a dialogue with all the souls who were involved in this. This allows the freedom of a collective of souls, who were also present at the same time. A forgiveness ritual to all those involved, also brings immense energy back into the ancestral field. This increases empowerment and a healing of the distorted field, which has been affected.

The role of some entities can be to try and take humanity or the individual away from the light of themselves and to feed negative thought forms into the collective. In the ancestral field, this feeds into the fields of the ancestors. Entities can be great teachers of what needs to be healed within ourselves and the collective healing; they have contributed to the journey of the soul. In the ancestral field the influence of entities has a magnificent impact because thousands of ancestors are connected to the ancestral fields of their bloodline. The opportunity to clear and liberate thousands of souls at a time through ancestral healing, demonstrates the importance of this work. Humanity has created an immense amount of its own shadow. However, the shadow aspect has always existed in the universe, the darkness within and outside of ourselves. Navigation of the ancestral fields helps illuminate our shadow and shows the reason for our challenges, the origin of which may be thousands of years ago.

Everything can be transformed and liberated, for those who choose to explore and heal in the divine timing. In some circumstances, entities can be transformed to continue their journey to the light. The present fast pace of the evolution of the planet also relies on the freeing of ancestral pain. Love is the energy which is raising consciousness on the earth, enabling more of the source-self to be held and embodied here on Earth. The power of shamanism lies in its powerful healing methods that can resolve and heal issues at a deep level. Many stars and planets have evolved to a level, where the shadow has less control in the everyday existence. The aim of the earth's evolution is to evolve to a similar level, which is also the journey of the soul. Freeing souls of entity attachments aids the soul evolution.

Origins of Entities

The origin of entities in the ancestral field can include the following:

1. Karmic past lives
2. Thought forms
3. Ancestral vampire energy
4. Curses
5. Earth bound spirits
6. Negative elementals

Karmic or Past Life Experiences

What we have been in our past lives and the experiences we have had, along with our ancestral connections, will always play out in our energetic fields. Our energy fields reflect our gifts and our shadow and the spiritual gifts we can show to the world. The energetic shadow needs to healed for our learning and soul evolution. There comes a time when we become aware of what needs to be healed which can be triggered in our lives by a repeating pattern in our ancestral fields. It can also be the case in ancestral work that we can meet the ancestral-self to learn and evolve. There can be an entity attached to the individual energetic field, connected to a lifetime when our ancestors or we ourselves experienced a great trauma weakening the energetic field. The energy fields can also reflect a lifetime when there was an abuse of power towards a person or humanity; leaving an imprint on our energetic fields and a possible entity attachment. The consequence is that we have other energies feeding into our thought forms, influencing individual behaviour, which continues down the ancestral fields. Memory is contained within the energetic fields and resolution of distortions enables the ancestral fields to reconfigure themselves, bringing back harmonic resonance, and reconnecting the ancestral lineage to harmony and balance.

Thought Forms

Thought forms rule our reality. They are very powerful energies that manifest according to the engine that is driving them with positive or negative results. There is an emotion attached to the thought form and the type of emotion attached drives the thought form. Thought forms can be related to an entity attachment. They are powerful energies that manifest a reality. The reality they manifest could be connected to an ancestral memory where a particular thought form was created. For example, thought forms can be connected to anger, depression and personality changes. They can also be connected to a past ancestral experience or a present life experience. In life, thought forms are always created naturally. However, if there is an entity attachment to a thought form, thought forms may be created that don't come completely from our own reality, but from the reality of the entity attached. Entities with negative energy will feed in very negative thought forms to the individual. It is detecting the thought form that may be having a negative impact on our life and any ancestral connection, which is the aim of ancestral healing. Our inherited ability to cope with the everyday stresses of life and trauma is also related to our inherited temperament which is directly related to what we have inherited from our ancestors. It makes sense that if our thought forms have been affected by an entity attachment through an ancestral connection, then similar patterns continue down generations. Entities time travel down the generations and so an entity will continue to be attached to the ancestor until it is healed and removed, freeing those also who are affected by this energy.

Ancestral Story
Panic attacks and fear

Mena suffered from panic attacks and thoughts around fear. Tracking down the ancestral lines, the ancestral healer found that this was connected to an ancestor who was separated from the family, due to an invasion of her village. The ancestor had to flee alone and the whole process of the journey to safety was full of fear and torment, until she found refuge in a neighbouring village. This trauma also resulted in an entity attaching to her energy field. This entity continued to feed in the thought forms of panic and fear. During the shamanic process, the ancestral healer removed the entity and reconnected this ancestor with the villagers she had left. Healing was sent and an energetic burial in the land of her birth, requested by the ancestor, was facilitated. This brought peace and harmony into the ancestral field. This helped to liberate the thought forms and trauma from Mena, which was connected to this ancestor's experience. Her panic attacks healed and she no longer had thought forms of fear.

Ancestral Vampire Energy

For many years I have observed the energy fields of clients and sensed that some had ancestral vampire energy attached to their energy fields. What was this I wondered? After a period of time, I realised this was an individual energy or collective energy whose vibration had become very low which was attached to the energetic field of the individual who in turn was energetically stronger. The energies were feeding off the light of other people because their own light was so low. There are a number of reasons for this. It could have been related to a collective of ancestors who had experienced a great trauma and so an aspect of their soul was stuck in this trauma. Their energy fields had then become so weakened that they needed to feed off energy of an ancestor who was holding the stronger light. Unfortunately, this had an effect on the living ancestor who may appear energetically weakened by this process. This energy could also be connected to dark energy. Ancestors who are connected to this type of energy and attached to the ancestor's weakened energy field are like energetic vampires that drain the energy field of the ancestor they attach to. During my ancestral healing work, I have freed and healed many individuals and ancestors of these particular energetic forms, so they have been able to continue their soul journey freely without energetic attachments in this form.

Ancestral Story
Constantly feeling stuck

A healer worked with Barbara who was dealing with issues of depression. She felt the presence of an ancestral vampire type energy attached to her energy field. During divination the healer connected to the spirit of a relative. The relative had been so wrapped up with guilt about murdering a person when she lived on the earth that her soul resided in an unpleasant environment on the astral plane and her soul was vibrating in eternal torment. She observed her in a field of negative energy that Barbara could not get out of. Her relative in this lifetime was ready to heal an aspect of herself, which was connected to this relative. By using her drum, the healer was able to show light to the relative and as a result the soul moved out of the darkness, and was able to move forward on the soul journey in the light, after a long period in a tormented environment. All this helped free Barbara from the energetic attachment in her energy field and the challenging feelings this had created. She felt less weighed down in her life and her depression lifted. Her feelings of stuckness and depression had been connected to the stuckness and depression of her ancestor.

Curses

The word curse is from the Anglo-Saxon word cursian, 'to invoke harm or evil upon'. Curses are described in more detail in Chapter 3. A magician connected to energy can send curses to other people, and also attach entities to these energies to further empower the curse. There can be a demonic phenomenon that transports entities and demonic tendencies, through a ration of genes that the second generation received from the first generation. Unfortunately, ancestral curses can be the most powerful curses and therefore require immense skill to break. The ancestral healer will need to track the origin of the curse, all the parties involved in the curse, and release any entities that are attached to this.

Earthbound Spirits

Earthbound spirits are souls stuck on the earth plane who have not moved forward on their soul journey; many of these earthbound spirits choose to remain on the earth. There can be various reasons which bind them to the earth plane. Spirits and those of ancestors who are stuck on the earth plane can sometimes attach and affect the energy fields of a person. They can attach if there is a resonance with the person or if there is vulnerability and a weak energy field because of trauma. Such entity attachment can move through generations of ancestors leaving an energetic imprint on the energy field. The story of this earthbound spirit needs to be heard and the soul released to continue their journey. Earthbound spirits can influence ancestors and so healing is needed to free such spirits from the ancestor's energetic field.

Other earthbound spirits can be ancestors who may have remained earthbound because of an individual or collective trauma, or being involved in something very dark against humanity. This affects an ancestor because this causes a distortion in the energetic field. Other spirits can remain earthbound due to sudden death, suicide, vows, or shame about what they did in a particular lifetime. When working with a client, an ancestral healer can track if issues are connected to a stuck ancestor, which is affecting their field of energy.

Ancestral Story
Poor relationship with parents

Susan went to see a healer because nothing was going right in her life and she wanted to improve her relationship with her parents. After divination the healer discovered that she had an earthbound spirit which had attached to her energy field when she had suffered trauma as a child. The entity was a man whose spirit had been stuck on the earth plane. The healer communicated with the spirit. This spirit attached his energy to the energy field of Susan because he wanted to protect her at a time when she was vulnerable and he was a very lonely spirit. Susan was ready to let go of this entity. The entity sought reassurance that she would be fine after he was released, which she gave, also asking for forgiveness. Susan spoke her forgiveness directly to the entity and the entity was released from her energy field and continued his journey to the light. Susan's own individual and ancestral field was liberated as was the ancestral field that the spirit was connected to. Susan's relationship with her parents improved dramatically after the healing.

Negative Elementals

Negative elementals can sometimes appear as dark bugs or astral tics and fleas. They can also be negative fairy beings, goblins or other negative elementals. They can be attached to spells, curses or thought forms. They do not have a mind of their own, but they can drain the energy field of the person they connect with. They can often attach to children who may have vulnerable energy fields caused by for example, trauma, and they can be invisible to the human eye. The negative elementals can affect the environment where a person lives and cause problems there. Shamanic processes both with entity release and space clearing can resolve such problems.

Ancestral Story
Suicidal tendencies

When Tina was a child, she had a vulnerable energy field due to having a very dominant mother, which caused her to feel depressed and vulnerable. As a child she spent considerable time in nature, which gave her much comfort during these trying times. Tina had many elemental energies attached to her energy field, which she was unaware of, and which had attached themselves to her when she was a child. In her adult life she had suicidal tendencies and often felt that many of her thoughts were not her own and on one occasion she nearly committed suicide. She was unable to pinpoint where these thoughts came from. She received ancestral healing and she released these elemental energies from her energy field. As part of the healing, Tina was also connected with an animal guide to help her feel empowered. She started using positive affirmations, enabling her to introduce more daily positivity into her life. The relationship with her family also improved

Demons

The word demons can instil the word evil. However, it is not always the case that evil is associated with a demonic energy. As described by the author Alfred Ribi in his book, *Demons of the Inner World*: "Demons are not by nature evil, our neglect of them and denial of their requirements, have made them evil". However, the author Carol Mack in her book, *A Field Guide to Demons, Fairies and Fallen Angels*, describes demons as: "Shape shifting talents and preference for concealment and indwelling and darkness". Demons can assume higher and lower manifestations, and they can control and dominate thought forms. They also have the power of illusion, which they sometimes use to trick other people to deflect from their true form. A demonic state results in the lack of compassion or connection to the human emotion. It is said that to get to the demonic state, energy is so wrapped up in guilt they cannot get away from the demonic form. There are often arch-demons connected to demons and these will feed in negative thought forms to the demons below them. This level of consciousness exists to try and manoeuvre humanity away from their light and source. Unfortunately, the ancestral fields of existence have contributed in many ways to the magnitude of this energy. Within this field there is immense trauma, abuse of power and feelings of being powerless. As the ancestral fields are vast fields of consciousness memories easily pass from one ancestor to another, as so does the influence of the demonic energy of lack of compassion or connection to human emotion for those affected. This of course, has an influence on humanity and how people relate to each other. The author Bruce Kapferer in his book, *A Celebration of Demons*, discusses that: "Human beings are subject to demonic power and the illusion of demonic power when they are disordered in themselves and their relations".

The association with evil has created a polarity of resistance of connection with these demons, which may be playing out in our energetic fields. Connected to the ancestral fields, demons can be other aspects of ourselves connected by the ancestors or our individual selves. Ancestral healing work has a role in making these projected aspects of ourselves conscious and therefore making them available to heal. It is important that these aspects become conscious because individual behaviours can be exhibited in a negative way, such as outward aggression due to the unhealed aspect of self, which is often connected to the ancestral field.

Entities have been around for a long time in the universe. There is the existence of demons and arch-demons. The arch-demon usually has an elemental energy attached to them. For those healers helping clients to release demons and arch-demons, they need to have strong skills and a strong connection to their spiritual helpers. Many entities have lost the connection to the light and do not have emotions. Healers need to be greatly protected when releasing these entities, as they can attach to energy fields that are very vulnerable, such as to people with addictions and the mentally ill. They can also contribute to creating addictive behaviour by the influencing of other people. Demons can hide within a home, remaining hidden and concealed. On occasions they can reveal themselves to perhaps scare the person who may be working to remove them. Their presence becomes obvious because they can work on people's thought forms and can cause disruption within the home. The presence of demons can also show itself by symptoms such as depression, negative thought forms, despair, and nightmares.

Ancestral Story
Alcohol addiction

Louise had a history of addiction to alcohol. She had an extremely traumatic childhood. Her mum was schizophrenic and did not nurture her children because of her inability to manage her symptoms effectively. The healer saw the client for a number of sessions completing different types of shamanic work. During a one-to-one session, the healer suddenly became aware of a big dark presence. Immediately her guides advised her to start drumming, which she did, and was guided to say the words: "Send it out and down". She felt a powerful energy move out of the body of Louise into the drum and this was released down into the earth. Louise saw a very dark entity released from her body, which disappeared via the drum. The healer's sense was that the entity attached to her due to her vulnerable energy field. Louise had a vulnerable energy field due to a traumatic childhood of living with a mother who had mental health problems and who had rejected her as a child. She had suffered from alcohol abuse due to the experience of this trauma but was in recovery. This healing helped her to move forward on her soul journey and to continue her alcoholic recovery.

Signs to Look for in Entity Attachment

The shamanic divination practice is an important practice to locate the origin of the problem in the ancestral field and the existence of an entity. There are symptoms to look out for that may show that there is an entity attachment. I need to emphasise that these symptoms do not always mean that you have an entity attachment. The symptoms along with other investigative work that is completed will identify if there are entities, this awareness is important. Please note that the identification of entities should be completed by an experienced healer.

Symptoms could include any of the following:

1. Mental health issues
2. Feeling drained and exhausted
3. Addictions
4. Disturbed sleep and nightmares
5. Uncharacteristic behaviour
6. Unexplained illness
7. Emotional problems
8. Thoughts that are not their own

These symptoms can be one or a combination; they can be recent or on-going.

1. Mental health issues
There are many different symptoms that are classed as mental health issues, including anxiety, depression, bipolar and schizophrenia.

The cause of mental health can be inherited and other factors such as trauma, can trigger the condition. Sometimes a person who has mental health issues has a vulnerable energy field, which can result in an entity attaching to them. There could also be an entity or entities passed down the generations, due to a past ancestral issue, such as a collective trauma or a curse put on the family. The ancestral healer can explore the story behind the mental health issue and release any entities that are attached to the person to enhance their life. The ancestral healer can also give advice to help any clients who have vulnerable energy fields.

2. Feeling drained and exhausted

Feeling drained and exhausted can be a sign that there is an entity attached, particularly vampire type entities, which drain the energy field of those people they are attached to. Exhaustion can also come from the type of entity that is attached to them, which can feed in negative thought forms, or can have a very low frequency, affecting the individual this is attached to.

3. Addictions

An entity attachment can create certain cravings and addictions, connected to the resonance of the entity, and the behaviour it creates. For example, the entitiy could be an earthbound spirit who wants to have experiences of these cravings and addictions again; such as smoking, or obsessional behaviour, or a constant pursuit of dark activities. The person is often unaware that this energy is the driving force in this behaviour. The release of the entity from the energetic field often results in the release of the addictive behaviour from the person affected.

4. Disturbed sleep and nightmares

A clear sign of an entity attachment can be recurring nightmares and dreams, including demons and other entities or dreams of being attacked. Awareness of this as soon as they start and prompt healing, makes it easier to remove these entities. This disturbed sleep is caused by negative thought forms and images that are brought into the dream state.

Ancestral Story
Distraught nightmares

A young client, Dora, had come to a healer because she was completely distraught. She was having constant nightmares of dark energy that she felt was trying to control her life. She did not feel in control of her own thoughts and was distraught that she had negative thought forms towards a close friend. During the session she tried to run away, and the healer had to coax her back. Immediately the healer realised she was in full possession of a very dark energy that was controlling all aspects of her reality. The healer completed the appropriate healing to release the energy form from her energetic field by bringing through powerful source energies of love via her drum. Immediately Dora felt calmer and at peace. The healer also gave her rituals to complete at home to keep her energy field strong. Dora is now happily present in her life and living in peace and happiness. The healer also worked on strengthening her energy field, which was vulnerable due to trauma as a child and her high spiritual gifts, which were not previously managed effectively.

5. Uncharacteristic Behaviour

A sudden change in behaviour, or behaviour that is not normally in the character of the person, can be a sign of an entity attachment. The energy of the entity could be playing out in the person's energetic field causing particular behaviour. Entities can interfere with behaviour either by feeding in negative thought forms, or inhibiting the person from being who they are.

6. Unexplained illness

Illness can happen at any time. There are some illnesses which may be baffling to treat or respond to, or an illness that sometimes may come out of the blue; this may be related to an entity attachment. Some entities carry the energy to create illness and these should be removed

7. Emotional problems

A series of emotional problems, or sudden emotional problems, may be the result of an entity attachment, which could be creating emotions beyond the norm. This may be connected to the energy of the entity that is attached to the person.

8. Thoughts that are not your own

Entities can feed in powerful thoughts if they are attached to a person who is vulnerable. This can cause havoc in the person's everyday life and also affect those people around them. Clearing these thought forms will enable the person to go back to their own thinking and behaviour.

Ways to Treat Entity Attachment

Treating and removing an entity must be completed by a healer who has been trained to avoid being energetically attacked by these energies and to protect the client.

Our soul evolution can only occur once we have mastered our own darkness or shadow and we are free of negative ancestral patterns, which no longer serve us. Entities have a role in helping to locate the ancestral story that has contributed to our behaviour or illness; the light and the dark need to complement each other. Humanity has created its own demons by its own destructive nature. This may have been caused by the destruction of the planet by wars and the mistreating of vulnerable people, or delving into dark magic.

Many illnesses in Africa are thought to be due to spirit possession. If a person has been possessed by a bad spirit, the traditional healer will work to cast out the bad spirit to stop the infighting between the person and the possessing spirit, which is affecting the individual. Indigenous cultures and our ancestors recognised the existence of entities and have transmitted this knowledge to the modern world.

Another method of healing involves smoking out any spirits which are possessing the patient, a process witnessed in Zambia. The method creates smoke, involving herbs and putting a cloth over the patient's head, so the patient breathes in the heavy smoke for five minutes to release the spirits. This releases the entity from the patient and the patient reports feeling better after the process.

My method of releasing an entity is part of the Ancestral Healing Practitioner Training that I have developed. I have trained healers to build up protection and a safe environment. This helps healers to connect to a spiritual guide who is a specialist in dealing with entities. The students have connected to incredible guides, who are very powerful and masters in their fields and who are able to deal effectively with entity attachments with compassion. For healers initiated into this process to release entities, they complete divination to find out all of that is contained in the ancestral field related to entities affecting the client and creating issues and complete the appropriate process to release them.

Ancestral Story
Smoking

Donovan had a very traumatic childhood and mental health had continued down the family on the mother ancestral line. He had smoked for more than 20 years and was keen to stop smoking.

During the divination the ancestral healer was shown that there was an entity in Donovan's energetic field, it was identified as a male earthbound entity. When the ancestral healer tuned into the energetic field of the entity, the entity showed a life, where there were belongings and he felt happy, joyful and peaceful. The entity had attached to Donovan's energy 36 years previously. The entity had attached itself to Donovan at a time when there was a void in his life. This progressively led to the addictive behaviour of smoking that Donovan developed later on in life.

After the divination, the ancestral healer proceeded to release the entity. When dialoguing with the entity, the entity stated that he was ready to go, but had wanted to be heard and listened to. The entity had attached himself to Donovan because he was longing to return to the time when everything was happy and peaceful and was longing to go back to that time. The entity expressed that he found it hard to let go and felt a bit sad and scared, however, he felt satisfied that he had been seen and listened to and had been held with love and compassion. The entity said he was sorry and that he did not mean to cause any harm. The ancestral healer told him it was time to return to the source and he agreed he was ready. Energy was sent to the entity and he returned to the source, and healing was also given to Donovan.

Donavan reported after the healing that he felt lighter and at peace. The next day he reported that he had stopped smoking. He felt liberated after the entity release and did not feel like smoking and had no cravings at all. He reported that he also could not stand the smell of nicotine anymore and never realised how "stinky" it was. In his own words he stated, "It has been two weeks since I have not smoked and believe me it is a miracle".

Step Into Your Own Power Exercise

Complete this exercise to empower yourself to step into your own power and to be more of who you are.

1. Write a note about when you have felt the most disempowered in your life. What were the circumstances, how did you feel, what emotions did you feel and how did you behave in the world afterwards? Draw an image to show this.

2. Write a note about how you would look or feel when you felt totally empowered. What are the emotions, how do you feel, and how do you behave in the world? Draw an image to show this image of you.

3. Meditate for 7 consistent days and call in the image of the empowered you into existence with love and harmony.

Ancestral Wisdom

Entities have always existed on the earth for the individual to learn from and evolve through. Entities are the manifestations of the shadow and the dark. Entities can be like a revolving door through which opportunities for real growth are possible. These energetic forms hold key information of wisdom that we need to grow, evolve, and learn from. From healing these aspects, we heal distortions in our own fields and those of the ancestors. There are different types of entities and we should always deal with these with respect. Experienced healers must be the only ones to release them.

Mastering of the entity field holds a key to reconfiguring the DNA and our own evolution. By illuminating the entities, you will illuminate what is hidden in yourself and humanity. Mastering these leads to a rebirth of the self. Do not judge anyone or the self for these entity attachments as they are a looking glass and an opportunity to aid the self and the ancestors. Where light is shone growth accelerates, in some cases for the entities too. They reflect what society has become, dysfunctional, and disconnected from the truth of self. Many entities are so wrapped up in guilt and control that they cannot get out of this awareness.

Love and compassion show a light that many entities have lost and provide an opportunity for hope. The power of love can break through barriers for many people who feel there is no hope. A light from an ancestral healer can ignite the spark of a connection they once knew. Shine the light of peace and love and many people will be able to transcend the darkness. Imagine the lights from the front of a car. These beams of light show a pathway, which is hidden in the darkness and so can be the source light, which helps entities to have a way out. We do not forget those who dwell in the shadows. We light a candle of peace and harmony for them so that they obtain the opportunity to move through the darkness. We approach entities with caution, but hold them in our hearts because many of them are our ancestors too.

Chapter 5

Collective Trauma: Humanity's Shadow

*Memory of cause and effect binds together the
ancestral dream, to behold the fate, which created
the trauma and created the collective memory.*

Collective Trauma

Collective trauma is interwoven and imprinted in our history. The collective unconscious will always play out in the energetic field of consciousness, because everything is interconnected. The web of existence contributes to the formula of life; we always learn from each other. This trauma is woven into history and often serves as something for humanity to look to and learn from. Patterns often repeat themselves, and within these is an opportunity for great healing for humanity, the ancestors and ourselves.

Groups often come together to form communities or to have a common experience. The dispersion of a close kin or family through a collective trauma has the impact of causing mass fragmentation and distortion in the ancestral fields. This inevitably leads to issues that feed down generations. Ancestral spirits are in the subtle time reality, an aspect of the extensive of what is contained in the subtle frequencies of our own lives. Subtle frequencies are frequencies, which are contained within spiritual energy. There are various archetypes that feed into a group to create a particular consciousness and this aspect binds an individual into a shared experience. These experiences link into the ancestral field. These collectives form together often unconsciously to have a conscious experience, both positive and negative.

The energy field of the ancestral lineage will adapt or configurate, depending on the experience that has taken place in the ancestral field. These can include groups that form together to go to war, live together in a community, and those who experience a trauma together. Such groups have a common spirit and a collective consciousness binds each group together energetically. It is often the case that when an individual soul who has been affected by a collective trauma is healed, other souls who have also been similarly affected by this collective trauma are also healed. The kin or family never forget each other when the opportunity to heal arises. This is the inherent nature of harmony and the love that people have for each other.

A collective consciousness can also be based on other factors, including coming together as part of a particular tradition; souls who have come together for a particular purpose; or a collective of souls forced together due to colonisation. There is a growing awareness of how trauma affects individuals and how collective trauma has an impact on the individual as well as the collective. Collective trauma in present and past lives have an effect on the ancestral fields that an individual is connected to. This trauma influences the energetic fields of ancestors and thus plays out in the ancestral fields.

The Distorted Human and the Abuse of Power

It has been well proven by many socialists and philosophers that a driving force in human behaviour for many people is the pursuit of glory. At times the pursuit of glory has lost control to the detriment of other people. The feeling of being powerful over other people is the energy that has created and contributed to collective trauma on the planet.

There is a great energy created from this, the energy of subordination and control of other people. This often involves active behaviour at the extreme end, gaining power, glory, control and material gain quickly, through the exploitation of other human beings.

Power plays out as an energy force that has been turned on its head. Every individual is inherently powerful. It is their divine right, but many people are made to feel powerless when confronted by a man or woman who is working with their power to cause harm to other people. The energetic thought form of the abusers of power is distorted in itself, magnified by the intensity of the focus on the individual need. There is also an energy created of great subordination, the looking down on other humans as more inferior and the need to control other people, by the instilling of fear or other mechanisms on people. The perpetrators of this abuse of power also affect the ancestral fields, by running this programme down the generations. This also feeds into the collective distorted field of the shadow aspect, this in turn allows other people to feed into and instill the same behaviours. Until there is a balance of living in harmony, love and respect for each other, this programme of instilling collective trauma on other people will continue. Some institutions and community structures have, on occasions, allowed such power abuse to continue and have contributed to mass collective trauma.

Kings

A king is described as the male ruler of an independent state, especially one who inherits the position by right of birth; there are also kings of tribes and nations. Kingship, a powerful position, is interwoven with being a director of other people to implement plans and wishes. There are many kings who have worked for the good of humanity and many who have abused their power and position to inflict misery on other people. Kings, like governments, acquire certain powers to be able to invade lands and create wars. A king is sometimes a man who leads his tribe or nation into war. He might be the person who decides when to make war and when to make peace. Wars, which can also be described as collective traumas, have played a great part in increasing the power of some kings.

An advantage of states that are organised by kings is that they are able to organise laws and groups. The stabilisation of monarchies is dependent on nationalism and commerce. The king psychology has to remain strong to prevent revolutions. On many occasions to the detriment of other people and to maintain control, nationalism and economic gain, they have implemented actions that have contributed to the collective trauma of other people, by exploiting them for personal and national gain. For example, in August 1518, Charles 1 King of Spain granted a licence for Africans to be sold as slaves in Africa and the Americas. Queens also act as heads of state and the same experiences as that outlined by a King ruler can manifest.

Governments

Governments create systems to manage communities and societies. They are linked to military power and the extent of military power is often the leveller on how they show and display their position to the world. However, the drive for economic power in many situations, has created wars and abuse of other countries and individuals to prop up the economy. In history, there have been invasions and occupations of other lands, which have resulted in trauma for the communities involved. There has also been the introduction of new cultures and beliefs from the invading country, which is different from the beliefs of the communities who lived on the land. Many landowners, who had inherited their lands from ancestors, were pushed away from their ancestral lands. The power of government is that it has the huge power to influence. Some governments can influence by negative propaganda that can impact on other people, and other governments can lead by corruption with their implementation of laws, with adverse effects on communities.

There are various collective traumas in history instigated by governments. For example, the Holocaust (1933-1945), which killed more than 6,000,000 Jews and torturing many more. Also, the atomic bombing of Hiroshima and Nagasaki in 1945 in World War Two by the United States, killing thousands of people and injuring many in horrific ways. There have been many collective traumas caused by governments and there are many souls who are trapped in this aspect of time by such collective traumas. These souls are waiting to be healed, freed and returned to harmony, and in turn they will also free and heal their ancestors.

Religion

The aim of religion is in one way an intention to create group cohesion and community, and many religions do create this and do well for their community. However, like other influential institutions with a great influence, there have been times when an abuse of power has taken place. There have been many religions over time, which have created dogma, as a means of creating control. Psychological manipulation is as powerful as physical manipulation which can have an influence on a collective. For example, vows of silence and celibacy from an ancestor as a result of being part of a religious group, can also affect an ancestor. The influence of religion on the ancestral field is immense. There are various different religions and this is related to culture. In many indigenous communities, the community communicated directly with the gods or through a medicine person. As religion has evolved, it has created religious officials and leaders who have held powerful positions and influence, and some members of religious systems have abused their power. Many religions have inflicted physical and psychological trauma on their members, which has continued down the generations.

Priests, Magicians, Shamans

There are many medicine men, the high priests and shamans who work for the good of all and some who work to create a controlled community by fear and manipulation. This is created by demonstrating power over matter or energy, which many people have the ability to do, for the good and also for evil. It can simply be to obtain status and influence and to control other people. Some leaders create a mechanism, to ensure that they obtain and enjoy power over their communities or followers. A few can be master psychologists, who from their power and influence create the energy of fear to control people. There are many in this category, who have genuine power of magic, working with spiritual forces and energy to harm and affect other people. There is also the impact of generational curses, which can affect ancestors in the ancestral lineage. In the source, there is also the energy of dark forces, which continue to feed into the collective, controlling, and manipulating where they can. They continue the cycle of energy that serves to influence other people to exert power and pain, continuing the cycles of collective traumas, which continue on Earth.

Ancestral Story
Ancestral displacement

John requested a shamanic journey to find out if there was displacement from his ancestor's ancestral lands. During the journey, the ancestral healer saw one of the spiritual guides showing a picture of a vast desert. The scene was of children and horses lying in a particular spot. They were frozen with shock on their faces. When the ancestral healer looked closer, there were boys around the age of 13, with the same look on their faces. All of them had been sucked down into the sand. The ancestral healer asked the spirit guide what had happened and he was guided to connect in with the client in the room. He instantly connected with his third eye and saw a channel of energy floating outwards, up and ahead of him. The scene opened and it was connected to a young woman who was in the desert watching the boys from a distance. She was traumatised, screaming and crying. This young woman was a twin of one of the boys and they were ancestors of the client, John. The ancestral healer in dreamtime automatically went to her, held her, and kissed her on her cheeks. She calmed down but she couldn't stop staring at the boys, her face wet with tears. The ancestral healer saw that there had been one boy leading the group who had purposely led everyone to this place in particular. He was quite cocky, knowing that this was a place of quick sand, but he defied the stories and warnings of the adults of the community and took the group there. Consequently, everyone died in the quick sand.

The ancestral healer asked the spirit guide what had started all of this and he stated that a medicine man in their village had sent the boys on a vision quest out into the desert. The young woman, who was the twin of one of the boys, had followed them because she felt she should also be allowed to go on the vision quest, not only the boys. The ancestral healer asked the spirit guide to take her to the medicine man, so she could ask him why he sent the boys there. The medicine man was in a white tent, dressed in white and had white painted patterns on his face. He said that he needed to get rid of the 'naughty' boy and this was the best way to do it; he spoke with no regret.

The ancestral healer returned to the dreamtime and to the quick sand with her guide. They helped the boys and horses out of the quick sand. Many were crying and all were scared, so they reassured them. The Healer sent the twin boy to sit with his sister, they held on to one another and the spirit guide put a protective dome over them. She asked if the children were all right and to bring the medicine man to them to apologise. They said no. The "naughty boy" had tears running down his face and said that he wanted to go home. She noticed his negative energy. He also had red eyes not black eyes and she saw that he was possessed. She began to take everyone back home with the spirit guide. but something felt wrong. Her guide told her that he needed to be returned to his 'equal' energy. The sky turned black to the west and *sucked up this boy. The healer began to take the other children home but something felt wrong. She didn't like leaving the child like this, so her spirit animal flew up into the dark cloud to where the boy had been taken and shot an arrow of white energy towards this, in that space the clouds turned white and the boy was returned to the light of the source. All the children were returned safely and the parents and the villagers came out to greet the children. This healing cleared the trauma that John's ancestors had experienced from his energy field, healing the feeling of displacement and disharmony connected to this trauma. John felt more centred and balanced after the experience.*

The Impact of Collective Trauma

Collective trauma creates particular thought forms that feed into the planet's shadow aspect. Collective trauma is trauma that is multi-generational and related to an accumulation of time. Therefore, it goes beyond the time when the trauma occurred. As such, past problems that have not been dealt with can become ancestral demons, which cast their shadow on the present and can influence the future. The individual is part of a collective ancestry, which feeds into the collective dream. That dream inspires or becomes a distorted dream, a dream of a distorted reality caused by trauma, which needs to be healed. What is written in the ancestral collective tablet of stone embeds and imprints in the ancestral collective field. This trauma binds a human to the consciousness which exists in humanity and inhibits the expansion of the soul. When humanity connects through experience with these aspects that disengage from the source self, there comes into play wisdom about how the earth's evolution and individual evolution has been stagnated and stuck in an aspect of consciousness. The effects of a collective trauma pass along the ancestral generations and can play out in different ways, ranging from ancestral illness or particular negative thought patterns. These fields also play out in the earth's consciousness, because there are usually similar thought forms or actions behind an action that has created a trauma.

The energy of thought forms of distortion plays out in the collective and attracts those people in resonance. From resonance is created a similar type of behaviour, i.e. the thought form of abuse of power, which will feed into the mind of those people who created this and thus the cycle continues. The response to collective trauma plays out in our energy fields dispersing energetic distortion across the generations. It causes fragmentation of the self and in the collective consciousness. Within each collective is a mechanism of transference, this is positive and negative. The ancestors through our bloodline have paved the way for our individual journey, evolution and planetary resonance and transferred memory down the generations.

The collective aspect of our inherent nature is imprinted within us and is part of our soul evolution. Collective trauma has the purpose of reconciliation because when we track the aspect of the self that has been part of the collective trauma, we heal an aspect of our soul. From this we reclaim the harmonious human and our selves. The collective consciousness at its highest level is that of oneness, we as individuals are a tiny part of the source consciousness. In many ways, one of the main consciousnesses that feed into the planet is the memory of the collective trauma throughout time. This has positive and negative effects on the earth's consciousness. There are negative thought forms that feed into the individuals affected by collective trauma which impact on soul incarnations until these are healed and resolved. Collective trauma binds together an energetic force or energetic entity that continues to play out in the ancestral memory and human consciousness in the collective.

There are codes of information that provide access to what may have been lost in an individual soul or collective. The memory of these need to be made available as a portal to one of the main aspects of the collective shadow, so renewal and healing can take place. Disharmony is the shadow aspect we learn from and continually evolve through. There is no escaping what is contained within our field of memory, be it of the victim, or the perpetrator. Collective trauma serves humanity's expansion, because it forms a bridge into different aspects of consciousness, light, and shadow. Holding an internal belief that there is only light, disengages the soul from part of the cosmos. The shadow is part of us. Engaging uncovers the individual and ancestral healing that needs to take place to release ancestral aspects, which no longer serve us as we move into true mastery of who we are at a soul level.

The source soul is a complex matrix of consciousness, linked to our ancestors. The re-birthing of the planet is not only connected to an individual soul, it is also a connected to a harmonisation within the ancestral line. An individual has the ability with the right ancestral practitioner to free many ancestors who have been connected to collective trauma, affecting the ancestral line. This is the energy that is available on the earth now, as it goes through a rebirth in consciousness. There are periods of time in the earth's history when collective trauma has existed and manifested, at times thousands of people losing their lives at the same time. Due to the frequency of the earth and a lack of harmony within humanity, collective trauma needed to have been in existence to serve the awakening of consciousness needed at this time. The collective wound becoming conscious needs to be looked at and healed. Healing the mass wound contributes to a harmonisation of the consciousness of the collective wound, and disharmony between individuals.

Awakening comes into play, by the call of the soul or the ancestors to heal the collective wounds, causing mass healing and a shift in consciousness. A shift in consciousness can be connected to experience, loss, awareness, and awakening. Humanity does not exist to battle the darkness or shadow. The resurfacing of the self from healing the collective wounds rebirths the self to another level of soul evolution. Clearing the collective wound clears energetic pathways within the self, inherited from the bloodline, enabling the soul to be freer to integrate more of the source self here on earth. This like a falling pack of cards helps humanity to hold more of the source-self here on earth. The alchemical journey is the resurrection and rebirth of the soul because through the shadow and dark experiences, comes evolution and transcendence into the next stage of the soul journey.

Effects of Collective Trauma

Collective trauma affects not only the mass displacement of the group, but also has effects on the individual souls within the group, as described below:

Accumulated Stress: the stress of being part of a collective trauma has a massive effect on the soul vibration, the memory of which the soul continues to hold. This can play out in a number of ways down the generations, including through feelings of anxiety and depression, not fitting in, and panic attacks. This in my view has an effect on genes that continues down the generations.

Displacement: being forcibly displaced from where you have been as a result of collective trauma has the effect of not feeling settled in one physical place and feelings of disconnection; feelings of never belonging anywhere; never having closure with ancestors; and feelings of abandonment and loss.

Burial: often collective trauma results in an appropriate burial not being given to a person who has died. Not being allowed to mourn collectively or individually and not being allowed to grieve has an impact. Not being given the appropriate burial in line with traditional beliefs leaves a soul unsettled. Buried on foreign land or not being given a burial at all, also creates feelings of not belonging and not being at peace.

Unresolved Trauma: this continues to play out in the ancestral fields compounding the person's feelings of the inability to move forward in life; and creating feelings of being stuck. This needs to be healed and closure made on a collective trauma and the trauma it has created.

Illness: this is created by distortion in the energetic fields. Inevitably, the collective trauma of ancestors causes a distortion in the energetic fields, affecting genetics and creating the manifestation of illness. Similar illness passes down the generations. For example, alcoholism continues down generations, along with other addictive behaviour.

Identification: lack of identity and fragmentation of the soul is created by being part of a collective trauma. This can also create problems of being dramatically disconnected from a culture, who a person is identified with. This can create confusion with identity; problems fitting in; and other expressed behaviour.

Oppression: collective trauma when exerted by other people often creates victims who are left powerless. Oppression is a powerful feeling that limits an individual in many ways, not allowing the person to move fully into the power of who they are.

Addictive Behaviour: many Native Americans died of alcoholism during colonisation because explorers introduced alcohol in exchange for various goods and as a means to show kinship and friendship and to control people. The cultural influence of the introduction of alcohol and the effect on the ancestral lineage has been proven to move down the generations. Introducing a substance that was not familiar to a culture, caused a distortion and consequently an illness manifested in the ancestors. Alcohol can create escapism by not allowing the body to feel pain or to remember. Traditionally alcohol moved people away from their cultural beliefs, these beliefs would have been used to heal, or manage, an illness or problem.

Ancestral Story
Not feeling seen by other people

Sean worked with an ancestral healer to look at the issue of not feeling seen that was evident in many of his ancestors on his father's line. The healer took him to a scene where three of his ancestors were slaves. Treated in terrible conditions, three of them were chained to each other. They were often made to kneel and not look up, always downwards away from their slave masters. They often used to look at the sky when they were able to and look at the birds and saw how free they were. They wished they had this freedom too. Sean sent healing to this scene to free them from this entrapment of their souls, they immediately stood upwards and released the chains that had bound them. In the room Sean heard beautiful sounds of the universe. The ancestors on his father's side came to greet them because they were freed to continue their soul path. They were all greeted with flowers and there was much joy and celebration. As this process finished, the ancestral healer saw a beautiful rainbow behind Sean. He really had crossed the rainbow bridge. He was also asked to wear a ruby stone in honour of his father's ancestors. Sean felt immense love and celebration for what the healer had achieved and both of their hearts were full of love.

Collective Trauma Throughout History

It is worth examining a period in time where collective trauma impacted on the ancestral field. This collective trauma, along with other collective traumas, continues to affect many people in different aspects of time. Take for example, the historical and present-day reality of slavery. The account of African slavery has all the information of trauma that affects all who are enslaved.

Slavery continues to exist. It is happening daily on the earth. The impact of slavery continues to feed into the collective. Slaves are dehumanised into objects by being bought and sold. The psychology of emancipation and being restricted has created many wounds on the ancestral fields. In African slavery this was a torturous life of existence. There were feelings of hopelessness and separation from families and the ancestral lines. Many people lived in the hope of being reunited with their loved ones, but never were.

The modern African slave trade began in 1441, before King Charles 1 of Spain issued his charter for slave transportation. It began with twelve Africans being kidnapped on the Guinea Coast and taken to Portugal as a gift for Prince Henry. In the 16th century due to economic circumstances, there was a massive demand for slave labour. As a consequence, there was an increase in wars, kidnapping and raids to obtain human slaves. This created a new opening because prior to this, slaves had been transported from Spain and Portugal to the Caribbean. It is well known that during a 350-year period, at least 10.7 million black Africans were transported between two continents and a further 1.8 million died during the journey. The slaves were taken to various destinations including North America, Brazil, the Caribbean and Europe. The slave trade was brought into the world by the aristocracy who were involved in supplying and selling slaves to merchants. These slaves were displaced and sold to land owners, and many slaves were also used by merchants. The energy and memory of these enslaved individuals is left in our quantum fields and affects many ancestors today.

Slave owners created various processes to control the slaves. This included breaking down their spirit and making them docile and easily manipulated into what they wanted them to do. This was a system of human exploitation, linked to the energy of one power over another and the need to exploit for money, economic, and personal gain. There are of course, also records of abuse ranging from rape and torture. The constant energy that was exerted by the slave owners brought down the power and spirit of those people they enslaved. The daunting story of the Igbo Landing, in Glyn County in Georgia, this was the site of the largest mass suicide of enslaved people in history. The slaves were captured in Nigeria and placed on a slave ship in 1803. There was an uprising and the captors were killed. However, the slaves were grounded and not wanting to be enslaved again the group committed suicide by walking into the waters of Dunbar Creek.

Ancestral history was affected by the slave trade. Many African cultures worshipped their ancestors for guidance and connection with them, to help feel empowered in their lives. They believed the ancestral spirits were always guiding their lives and the ancestral spirits were worshipped and honoured in ceremonies. The power of the ancestors considered the most powerful were those who died the longest time ago. Slaves were taken away from their family lands and thus disconnected in many ways from the spirits of the land, which they felt were important for their spiritual connection. They were also taken away from their communities. In many ways, slavery served to disconnect individuals from their ancestral spirits and ancestral connection. The author Booker Washington, in his book, *Up From Slavery*, describes how he was born a slave on a plantation; his ancestors on his mother's side were brought from Africa to America. His father was a white man on a nearby plantation. As the result of being born a slave, he knew nothing about his ancestry because there was no attention given to family records or family history of slaves.

Many slaves were alienated and isolated. They were not treated as human beings, but as objects to be exploited and abused. Millions of people and the ancestral lineage continue to be affected by this mass collective trauma. There is debate on the extent to which African culture was preserved when the slaves were taken to other lands. Many scholars argue that this was preserved while others argue not. However, within the inherent culture are imprints of this trauma, which have moved onto current generations, expressing itself in various ways.

Fear. Fear was a technique used to ensure slaves did what they were told. Fear remains in the cellular memory and passes through generations who feel this. Fear is like a law of attraction, which attracts what it gives out. So, while this is in the energy field, it will attract that what instils fear or creates fear. Many people died a terrible death, or witnessed terrible deaths when collective traumas occurred. Fear is a powerful thought form which will have impacted on the energetic field and the ancestral fields. A result of this is a weakness in the energetic field. This makes individuals vulnerable to other energies, illnesses and affecting life on many levels.

Victims. All slaves were victims, taken out of their environments and becoming victims to a life of enslavement beyond their control. Being a victim attracts the energy of someone wanting to gain power over that victim. This could also attract entities and the affected person may have an energy field that is vulnerable to other energies trying to enslave and over-power. A victim creates the energy of feeling like a second-hand citizen, always enslaved and abused by another and so this feeling continues down generations.

Anger and Frustration. Slaves often felt anger and frustration. Angry at how they were taken from their homes; angry at not being in control of their lives; and angry at the abuse they were experiencing. Anger is a strong emotional state and no doubt contributed to distorted energy fields. This may have contributed to illness, which continued down the generations. Thoughts of being enslaved, restricted in movement and claustrophobia were also common, along with feelings of not being able to move forward in life. Slaves do not feel in ownership of themselves and these are thought forms, which may have continued down the generations, creating similar behaviour.

Ancestral Story
Feeling trapped

Debbie asked the ancestral healer journeying to the upper world, to see whether there were any ancestral collective traumas affecting her. The ancestral healer reported entering a luminous, stony passage with arches. She saw someone running in fear. He ran to the end of the passage and was stuck at a wall. He began to think, "I need to escape". A light began to enter the passage from a small space at the top of a wall. The person felt suffocated and a dark energy started moving towards the person, an entity that was trying to connect with the client's traumatised ancestor.

The ancestral healer saw slave boats filled with naked men who only wore an orange bracelet. They were all feeling dizzy, soulless and were bumping into one another like the living dead. She saw a vision of Mother

Africa and saw the west coast of the continent and also people being sucked away. Every person was like one of her tears being sucked away. The ancestral healer asked how all of this could be healed and Mother Africa said; "It was much bigger than this and all of the stories inside needed to be expressed and told to the world". The word that kept coming up was 'honouring'.

Returning to the scene of the tunnel, the ancestral healer connected with Debbie's ancestors. He said he didn't want to escape; he only wanted to be at peace. She saw Debbie holding the ancestor in dreamtime and the ancestor turned into everyone who was there at that time as slaves. Debbie helped to heal the scene by putting her hand on her ancestor's third eye and all became peaceful. She was honouring, holding and being non-judgemental and this automatically in that journey healed her ancestor. There was no anger, only honouring and peace. The ancestral healer saw how there was acceptance from Mother Africa, like a red pulsating heart. There was no sadness, only love as a power. What she had experienced was loving consciousness with the third eye, telling people to raise their consciousness.

Debbie has reported since the healing that she has been extremely open and emotionally alert, grounded with a clearer vision, but also has a sense of melancholy. A big shift and whole-body cleanse worked through her system as the result of this healing.

Collective Trauma Release Exercise

Find a quiet space. Light two candles, one to represent your mother's and your father's ancestral lines. Connect to your heart and connect to the energy of love within your heart, and state the following ancestral prayer.

Ancestral prayer
For my mother's and father's ancestral line
affected by collective trauma
Ancestors we honour your path that left you intertwined
with other people; it was destiny we know
I send love and light to heal your wounds
To heal your pain
To help free you from that which binds
I send the energy of love and light to lift your soul, with all its might
So that you are free to return to the source
To continue your journey
Healing the pain within you
Always with love and harmony
And so it is.

Give thanks and blow out the two candles to complete the ritual.

Ancestral Wisdom

Collective trauma has contributed to a distortion in the DNA of many ancestors. Geneticists recognise the influence of the environment on gene behaviour. I feel that this has been a major influence on behaviour and similar illness that manifests down the generations. Tracking the connection between an issue and an ancestral collective trauma not only heals the individual, but also can heal and free many ancestors and souls. From one healing, thousands of souls also could be freed, who may have suffered a similar trauma at the same time.

Being aware of the behaviour that creates collective trauma helps to understand why certain behaviour continues down the generations, that of perpetrator and victim, all will play out in the ancestral field. Memory serves us well. We can learn from this, no matter how traumatic it is. We can also be shown ways that are different. Awareness enables recognition of similar behaviour that is being created and harnesses mechanisms to defend against it. Profound healings from this awareness can take place. This can help cure illness and behavioural patterns. This will also have an impact of healing thought forms such as fear, which are having an adverse effect on humanity.

When we merge with all the fragments that are missing, due to the entire collective trauma, we can create the evolution of the new human a call back and harmonisation of the energy of destruction. The energetic makeup of the source is oneness and for that we strive in all of our relationships, including those with our ancestors.

Humanity for too long has been driven by greed, power, and money. These factors exist to help the individual or a small group of individuals. This also creates certain behaviours as the individuals operate to maintain the status quo. This mindset serves to create more trauma and disconnection because the driving force is self-survival and control. This can be broken by a different mindset being applied to what is important in life and more awareness of how this behaviour affects other people.

The collective dream is the individual dream. What priorities the collective has particularly by those people in power, helps shape the environment and the lives of other people. As the nature of the earth fights for survival, there is no doubt that unless the focus of humanity changes, there will be more people who suffer from the adverse effects of collective trauma. The effects are an earth that in the long-term will struggle to survive.

Reflection time

*Write your insights, healing and tasks moving
forward to continue to heal your life.*

Chapter 6

Individual Trauma: Lessons from the Ancestors

We swayed, we fell, we resurrected into the arms of those we choose for our evolution and learning.

Life begins with two parents, mother and father. Every time a child is born, not only does an ancestor return, but the weight of the ancestral baggage also returns. The embodiment of the feminine and masculine energy is a universal plan, to bring harmony and balance to the individual and the planet because both energies are needed. It is also important for this energy to be embodied because it influences the energetic imprint of the DNA and it is what makes us human. The plan is the embodiment of the divine human on Earth, the embodiment of the source-self that manifests the source energy of unconditional love. However, the ancestral lineage we are part of contains many distortions in the fields of the masculine and feminine. This is caused by various factors that have taken place in the ancestral lineages which transmit down to the individual. Other factors which contribute to this are what has been inherited from the soul's individual journeys. The divine plan is for these to be healed and brought into harmony and balance within the self.

Personalities develop from the experiences with the mother and father and from this inherent propensity. Much of this is hidden in a complex web of existence; past, and present. Parents form our roots, our formula for life; imprints that show and guide us to what needs to be healed. How we choose our mothers and fathers is a karmic plan based on a number of factors, of both the individual and ancestral soul journey. The family is held together by a number of components, duty, psychological and emotional factors. Relational trauma is powerful and contributes to behaviour and emotional patterns that continue down the generations.

The journey of learning and evolution is witnessed through this dynamic relationship of nurture and abuse. What we experience in the mother and father relationship, forges a large aspect of the behaviour of the future. Building a therapeutic bond of love and harmony in the early years is considered particularly important. How this plays out in life is related to what persistent patterns move down the ancestral fields over eons. This is often related to the effect of the relationship that the parents had with their parents, along with tracing in the ancestral field as to how the origin of any problems manifested. The direct focus of many therapies and healing is the child and parent dynamic, which is powerful work, but delving deeper into the energetic fields of time in the ancestral fields, reveals a complex dynamic that plays out over time. Within this field are also the dynamic of parents who are working out their own ancestral patterns, trauma, and relationship. A child born into such a dynamic is working through a very complex programme for healing, awakening and transformation.

Ancestors and the Healing Journey

Trauma fragments energy and leads to behaviour that is a learned way of reacting to the effect of the trauma that has been experienced. The trauma creates destructive patterns and behaviours, which occur in various ways. These have an influence on the individual's life and those people around them. Within the individual soul field there is also a timeline of experience, which has contributed to present behaviours and dynamic. The aim is to heal persistent patterns that may exist down the timeline and also to heal the karmic relationship, along with ancestral patterns. How the individual heals is important so the ancestral traits do not continue down the generations.

Individual trauma, which is experienced in the present life is linked intrinsically to memories of the past at a soul level and programmes from the traits of the ancestors. What comes into play is a programme of behaviour externally and internally to reflect this field of memory. The playing out of this is to accelerate our healing and learning, along with an opportunity to embody more of our source-self, free of the influence of ancestral patterns that have existed down the generations. When we are faced with distortions in our ancestral fields, our spiritual growth is dependent on how we heal these, along with an opportunity to heal inherited illness and patterns.

Trauma was created by humanity, when people deflected from being in harmony with each other. This deflected from the truth of how human relationships should be. It all became about individual need, rather than collective need. Down the ancestral timelines, the trauma continued down the ancestral lines of those people affected, creating more fields of trauma. Neurological and emotional factors affected DNA imprints and a combination of various factors influenced the same behaviour to continue. Within the soul memory exists what needs to be transformed, and so the mother and father are chosen as part of that journey. When we experience and become aware of our programming, we take a spiritual soul pathway to experience, learn, and manage various karmic factors that the soul has engineered.

As a collective, we have contributed to the creation of many diseases, the destruction of the earth and negative aspects of consciousness that feed into our ancestors and beyond. Every journey of the experiences with a mother and father, is a major factor that can recreate the destructive patterns and behaviours that were the result of individual experience. Re-emerging and coming out of these behaviours is about tapping into ancestral wisdom, to seek and to heal the origin. This removes this energy from creating similar patterns in the future. This results in behaviour that will serve not to mirror the past but to give resurrection to a new future, clear of the past.

There is a need to balance the masculine and feminine within ourselves to help us individually have balance within ourselves and also to help with how we relate to other people. How this is balanced within us, is related to the influence of the mother and father and also how the balance of masculine and feminine energy has been handed down the ancestral lines. This is affected by how the ancestor's journey has been in relation to any particular trauma.

There are trigger points of repeated patterns down the ancestral lines, influencing the individual ancestor. It is like a dynamic mechanism that shouts out to be healed and transformed, a creation that from its origin repeats, until the divine timing to free all who have been affected by this pattern occurs. Individual trauma can be a repeated story that the individual soul or the ancestors have experienced, until one of the ancestors takes the courage to free themselves from this. At the same time ancestral help is needed to free the ancestral collective who held a similar trait and pattern. Many souls have chosen to take on this heavy burden to free particular patterns from their ancestral lineage forever.

Different Types of Individual Trauma

There are different types of trauma that cause a continuation of patterns down the ancestral fields. It is reflective of a complex web contained within the ancestral fields. At its origin, there are fascinating stories of interactions between humanity, which in its negative aspect has created repeated patterns and behaviours that repeat in the generations. A skilled ancestral healer heals them at its origin, sometimes tracking back in time for thousands of years via divination. Gifted healers can heal a distorted thread that sends a signal down the generations and to the DNA to free the past and future generations of this behaviour, to obtain harmony and balance.

Physical Abuse

Physical abuse is defined as any intentional act causing injury or damage to another person or animal by way of bodily contact. Abuse creates a high level of trauma. Survivors of abuse can be left with a variety of emotions; these can include feeling powerless, angry, traumatised, depressed, and disempowered. Damage from abuse is largely neurological because it causes brain and nervous system changes, which leave victims vulnerable to depression, addiction, and post–traumatic stress disorders.

Psychological Abuse

Psychological abuse is described as an infliction of mental anguish, involving actions that cause fear of violence. It has been found when a child or adult suffers abuse, particularly when experienced from a narcissist, it can cause shrinkage in the hippocampus and an enlargement in the amygdala part of the brain. Narcissists, for example, can be kind one minute and cruel the next. Psychological abuse feeds in negative thought forms, which manifest as more negative thought forms from the affected individual. These negative thought forms feed into behaviour displayed by the affected individual to other people and also influences the individual in terms of their relationships and their functioning in everyday life.

Sexual Abuse

Sexual abuse is described as any kind of sexual behaviour by an adult with a child, or any unwanted or inappropriate sexual behaviour from another child. It can also affect an adult. This abuse is extremely traumatic affecting the survivors into their adult life. Often this experience can be blocked out of a person's memory and feelings. The abuser abuses their position of being at the time in a more powerful position than the victim to carry out sexual abuse. The effects on the victim can include flashbacks, and extreme emotional behaviour, including anger, frustration and panic attacks. The survivors can also have blocked memories, which mean they shut down part of their emotional body. Sexual abuse is an abuse of power in one way or another in a relationship. Sexual abuse can happen against a child or an adult. Survivors of this abuse sometimes believe they were responsible for the abuse they experienced.

Symptoms of Individual Abuse

Dissociation

When a child or adult has experienced trauma, they can dissociate. The symptoms of dissociation are that the person can retreat within themselves. This is a coping mechanism, which allows a child's mind to withdraw from abusive circumstances and this abuse mainly starts in childhood, although adult experiences can create similar circumstances. Due to what a person has experienced or is experiencing, they separate part of themselves from what is happening and from the emotional experiences. As part of the dissociation, archetypes can be created which hold different memories and feelings. When an individual dissociates, they can detach from their environment. The extent to which they detach from their environment, can vary in moderation from mild to severe.

Entities/Possession

Experiencing abuse can make someone more vulnerable to entities or possession due to their weakened energy field. These entities can create thought forms in the affected person that are not their own and keep a person from being in their own source of power. This also creates a weak energy field that makes a person more vulnerable to attracting negative energies, challenging and negative people in their lives. This can make their problems worse and create repeated patterns. The energies that attach, keep the vulnerable person in a negative and vulnerable state of existence. This is a revolving cycle that creates repeating patterns and illness, until the person is healed of this aspect.

Negative Thought Forms

Being abused often creates negative thought forms. This can be towards other people or directed towards the self, for example thought forms around a lack of trust in other people. Such negative thought forms are powerful and hard for the person to heal from. Thought forms can be, for example, feelings of not feeling good enough, hatred of self and other people. These thought forms create an outlook by the individual, which is filled with hopelessness and a lack of insight for a better future. They weaken the energy field and can often create a negative impact in relationships. They can also lead to depression and create other illnesses in the body.

Anger

Anger is powerful energy; it can cause destruction on many levels to other people and to the self. Feelings of anger accumulate in feelings of rage and hatred and are common after an individual has experienced trauma. This anger can be directed at other people or internalised, which can lead to other issues and problems. Anger affects how we relate to each other. It can create illness if not expressed and healed. Certain triggers can cause this anger to be released, sometimes resulting in violent behaviour towards other people.

Ungrounded

A person who has experienced abuse can be very ungrounded, meaning they are not feeling connected to the body or the earth. The person has experienced so many traumas that they find it hard to be grounded in their body and often do not want to be in their bodies because they find it too painful. Being ungrounded contributes to a person feeling less embodied in their body and being less able to face their emotions. This also contributes to the experience of not having to feel their emotions, or their physical body. The feeling and need to feel ungrounded can lead to addictive behaviour or even mental health.

Disempowered

Abusers can often be bigger in size than those people they have abused or be in a position of power, leaving the victim powerless. When we are in our full power, we have clear boundaries. Boundaries are there to protect us physically and emotionally. When we feel disempowered, we feel vulnerable. This vulnerability makes us susceptible to further abuse or exploitation from other people. We can also give off the energy of being the victim, displaying feelings of being powerless and not feeling powerful. Feeling the victim can be an ongoing problem after being abused.

Illness

Trauma can create illness. Our emotional bodies and thought forms create our reality. Trauma contributes to many illnesses. Mental health is one illness that can come from trauma. Other conditions include anxiety, addictive behaviour, obsessional behaviour, and suicidal tendencies. Illness is created by many factors and ancestral influences are a very strong factor. There is scientific evidence of inherited illness and similar illnesses down the ancestral lines. At an individual level, what is contained in the ancestral line can be a trigger for an illness that is experienced. Individual trauma expresses itself in behaviour and the embodiment of the illness that is experienced. Trauma affects the nervous system.

Ancestral Story
Mother and daughter relationship

Joan experienced a trauma from her mother/daughter relationship. She felt that her mother loved her sister more than her. She felt unwanted in the family and she felt that she was not allowed to exist. This left her feeling lonely and depressed. A few days prior to completing her ancestral healing, Joan got a kidney infection. The last time she had experienced a kidney infection was when she was a child.

During her ancestral healing, the ancestral healer discovered that in a previous lifetime, Joan had been stabbed in the kidney, pushed overboard a boat and died by drowning. In that lifetime, she had been betrayed by a jealousy connected to someone in the family, leaving her with a certain legacy.

Joan was given healing and the energetic chords that had been attached to her, as the result of this were healed. After the healing, the kidney problem got better. Fear in Chinese medicine is connected to the kidneys. After the healing, she also decided to quit her job and spend more time with her grandparents on her mother's side. She let go of her fear and started to continue the steps of healing the mother's ancestral line.

Shame

Shame is usually understood as being a painful feeling of humiliation or distress, caused by the consciousness of wrong or foolish behaviour. Individual trauma can often result in feelings of shame. This creates internalised negative thought forms about the self, feelings of embarrassment, inadequacy, and sometimes guilt. This can affect daily life and interactions with other people and relationships.

Mother Wound

The foetus in the wound is affected by the physiological conditions that the mother creates. For example, it is known that infants born to mothers who are chemically dependent often present as critically ill and there are many psychological studies that show the influence of the mother/child relationship. For example, the author John Bowlby showed evidence that the deprivation of the maternal influence in a child's life caused substantial stress to infants and children, which affected them for the rest of their life. Mothers are seen by society as the main nurturers and when this does not happen it affects the child in many ways. The manifestation of the mother wound down the ancestral field, creates a distortion in the divine feminine energy. This is there to provide the divine spark to the feminine aspect. The role of the mother is to birth the qualities of the divine feminine to their children. The feminine wound transmits to the feminine aspect of the self, to the male and female lineage that the mother gives birth to. There are always of course positive aspects transmitted down the ancestral line but in terms of ancestral healing, it is the mother wound that needs to be looked at and healed to restore the divine feminine to the self. The mother gives birth and through her blood creates the feminine energy that transmits to her children. In its divine aspect, this energy is there to provide qualities of nurture, empathy, emoting, and compassion.

Nurture: includes the qualities of caring, encouraging, and protection, along with being taken care of during a period of growing, development, and support. This positive quality is one that provides a wonderful energy so needed in modern society. Caring for one another is one of the qualities needed to restore harmony and balance on the planet. The transmission of this quality down the ancestral lines is important for how humans interrelate with each other for harmony and balance.

Empathy: is the ability to be able to share feelings with another person and understand what they are going through. To get to this state, an awareness and understanding of another person's feelings and emotions are needed. It is also about having the capacity and ability to place oneself in another's position. This is an important quality to have because it develops an understanding of what someone is going through and why they may be reacting a certain way. It is a quality of compassion to show another human being.

Emote: is described as the ability to show emotion in a way that makes it very clear what you are feeling. Expressing our emotions clearly and in a sensitive manner, helps create a productive way of human relating. Connecting to the divine aspect of this level of communication in every day relating, improves and creates a more positive outcome in relating and prevents misunderstandings.

Compassion: means co-suffering and involves feeling compassion for another human being. It is a precursor to empathy. A person demonstrates that they are acting with care and kindness to another person. Kindness aids people to get through difficult times. Acts of kindness to other human beings creates less suffering and spreads a concept that can be brought to other people.

When these divine feminine qualities are out of balance there is less compassion towards each other. There is also less understanding and acceptance of the differences between others. There is more individualism and caring for self, rather than other people, which often means that when emotions are expressed it is not always clear what they are. This can cause other people to be upset or feel misunderstood.

Ancestral Story
Family trauma at time of birth

Mary's mother was born at a time when her grandmother was deeply unhappy. She had married a man she loved deeply and they had a daughter soon after marrying. It was during the post war times and they lived with her mother, four other siblings, their spouses and their new babies. The house was overcrowded and it was very stressful and volatile. She found herself pregnant again only months after giving birth to her first child. She was upset and distressed because she feared she was going to have child after child and live in poverty like her mother: Mary's grandmother was one of nine children. They could not afford a place to live and she knew her mother was an unwanted child because her mother had told her often. Mary was also another girl, her father favoured boys as did her grandfather. Her grandmother also described herself as an unwanted child; she was the eighth child and a girl. While pregnant, she found out her husband was having affairs with multiple women and one was also pregnant. She was devastated and wanted to leave him but could not afford to. They stayed together but she refused to have any intimacy with him for many years.

Unfortunately, Mary's mother had been sexually abused by her grandfather. Although she had no clear memories of the event, she started to have flashbacks after the age of fifty, which explained why she had been a deeply unhappy teenager who felt suicidal, self-harmed, suffered from bulimia, and was fearful of sex and intimacy.

Mary's father was a flirt and womaniser, so her mother would not leave his side and they argued constantly. Her mother frequently stormed out of the house in anger or distress because he was unfaithful and did not return for long periods of time. Mary's mother and her sisters could not wait to leave home as soon as they were able. While training for a job Mary's mother met her husband, a very charming, very handsome liar, and ultimately unfaithful, like her father and the pattern continued. She became pregnant and they married. Her father was pretty much absent, unreliable, emotionally abusive, and refused to work and consequently they were poor. Mary's mother left him and the marriage did not last a year.

Due to the trauma of childhood sexual abuse, her mother was unable to show affection, was emotionally disconnected, displayed huge disassociation, had body shame, was constantly dieting, and was intermittently bulimic. She was also very angry and lashed out. She was unaware of Mary's needs, physically and emotionally and was totally chaotic and Mary had no routine, no meal times nor bedtimes. She was frightened and was easily alarmed by everyday events that were presented to Mary. Mary's mum felt that the world as a frightening place, where all social situations were difficult and Mary was unaware of social rules and skills.

Mary's mother was totally disassociated from the world and everyone in it and this was the world in which she was brought up. Mary took responsibility for her unhappiness; her unexpected mood shifts, the daily chaos and the dramas. She felt it was her fault and she had to keep the peace. Mary also took on responsibility for her mother's stress and anxiety, displaying a role reversal as well as having to meet her mother's emotional needs, which were constantly changing.

Mary, despite being in a loving and supportive relationship with her husband, felt suppressed and felt that she was not seen or heard. She believed her husband was guilty of every possible male vice and viewed him with distrust and suspicion. Despite never giving her any reason ever to feel that way, she felt she was operating in a negative relationship; when in fact the opposite was true. This led to unnecessary conflict, irritation, sensitivity, lack of unity, and a division between the two of them, especially regarding the children. Mary had a sense of being trapped in an unsatisfactory marriage for the sake of her children.

Mary recognised many unhappy marriages within her mother's line of ancestors, which were strongly bonded together, but were bitter and resentful to each other. There was conflict around money and control; it was a dynamic of male versus female, unable to express love. Her ancestors were unable to resolve the conflict and distrust, but they would not separate or divorce. Children and family were often cited as reasons to tolerate the status quo, even when children are adults and no longer in the marital home. Children seem key to the dynamic and a tool for manipulation and control. However, Mary's mother did leave her bad relationship and got divorced. It was a very bad relationship and would never have worked, which her mother recognised, but she felt a deep sense of failure for not staying and for being a divorcee.

A healing divination was conducted for Mary, which revealed that the issue revolved around curses, spells, vows, and past lives. At some time in her mother's ancestral line a visiting priest was sexually abusing the children. One parent was aware of what was happening and the other parent was not, which was the start of the conflict between them and their having to stay to protect the children. The journey through the ancestral line and information provided from the spirit guide, revealed that *this pattern of abuse had already been broken by the separation of Mary's parents.*

At the start of the healing journey, Mary saw her back full of spikes like a porcupine. She felt this was because she was protecting her children, from the ancestral negativity and stopped it with her back. The healing involved removing the spikes and healing the area. She was given healing and felt her DNA reset. During the healing journey animal guides of a white dove and pigeon appeared. There was also an energetic chord healing process with the priest who had caused the abuse. At the end of the healing Mary saw a white owl in flight. Mary has reported feeling totally healed and peaceful by her ancestral shamanic healing journey.

Father Wound

The male figure is viewed as the protector, the one who will keep us safe and provide security: when this does not happen it shatters this belief system, which can affect relationships and the masculine energy within us. The masculine is a driving energy that moves us forward and gives strength and determination to all that we do.

Strength: everyone needs inner strength which is an important part of our coping mechanism. It helps to move through life ups and downs and to stride forward. It also helps with resilience and empowerment.

Driving energy: this energy helps to move forward and gives strength and determination to all that we do. This energy helps to move through obstacles and challenges in our lives.

Determination: keeps a focus on what we need to achieve. It is a driver, which keeps us moving forward in our lives and it reduces apathy.

Action: is a process of doing something to create an outcome. Action is a motivating force that helps us to create something in our lives, or to deal with something.

Ancestral Story
Father/daughter relationship

Angela's relationship with her father had always been complicated. He was an amazing father during her early years, always ready to play with her. He taught her to love nature, to understand the natural world, and they explored the woods and the mountains together. She had all types of pets growing up, from dogs to chicks, to blackbirds and eels. However, his relationship with her mother started to deteriorate when she was born, he was a fun father but an absent husband. He was also a person who liked to take chances and follow his dreams, sometimes following his dreams blindly. He would decide on a course of action and not consider the consequences for those people around him. Also, he was easily fooled by those people who preyed on his goodwill and blind ambition. When he decided to open his own business against Angela's mother's advice, he immersed himself in debt and ended up bankrupt. Eventually, her parent's relationship came to an end when Angela's father confessed that he had been seeing another woman for more than five years. Angela was ten years old at the time of their divorce and from that point on her relationship with her father changed completely.

Two years passed until she saw him again. She remembered not calling him dad anymore. She was always caught between the need to be perfect for her father, but at the same time misbehaving to have his attention and somehow the confirmation that he loved her enough not to give up on her no matter what she did. For many years, she was unable to speak with him, even though she always had so much she wanted to tell him. She said it was as if the words were stuck in her throat and she completely blocked her expression. Later in life when she became a mother the relationship improved, they drew closer again and were able to speak about the past. But then something horrible happened which made them separate again.

Angela received healing for two major issues. The first was in regard to a pattern that all the men on her father's side of the family had lovers outside of their marriages, with several children from different mothers. During the healing session the information was received that the origin of this behaviour was ancient and had to do with the fact that during many generations Angela's male ancestors had lost their families multiple times, due to war, famine, and disease. This triggered the instinct to have many children and many wives to ensure that the ancestry continued.

Through shamanic journeying Angela has been able to revisit the past and connect to her ancestors, to learn how to let go of this trauma and the behaviours that are an expression of it. The guides taught her how to use her menstrual cycle to cleanse and let go of the feelings connected to this trauma. By doing so, she felt she was able to be more present in the moment and feel more rooted. The unexplainable feeling of deep sadness and loss that she often felt was released and let go. She felt empowered and with more knowledge of her own self and the links that connect her blood to the past. She discovered a deep and ancient connection to the Celtic traditions and she was able to release and access ancestral knowledge that was once lost.

The second issue that was addressed during the ancestral healing was sexual assault to the children of the family. During this session her ancestral healer discovered that it was the presence of her stepmother who was the catalyst for both events, since she was already in her father's life when Angela was assaulted as young as four years old. She discovered that she used sexual energy and completed spells to achieve her goals, since she was incapable of love. It was this energy that attracted the sexual assaults. It was perceived that this was an issue that had been happening for many generations and as long as no one spoke about it, it would keep on happening. Many children in her family had been victims of sexual abuse, including her father, but none were ever able to tell their tale. Angela tried to do it by telling her maternal grandfather, but he told her never to tell anyone else.

Since the ancestral healing Angela has been able to work on herself in ways that were not possible before. She became able to connect the dots between the assaults she suffered and the feelings she had towards her body. It is an ongoing process.

As for the relationship with her father, Angela has left the door open for him. If he wished to return, she would receive him with love. Her connection to the ancestral knowledge has taught her that she can only control her own choices and that she has to be patient and accept the choices of other people, without fear and without regret.

Angela continues to receive new spirit guides and knowledge about how to protect herself and her family. Painting has also helped her because she uses art to manifest what she cannot put into words; sometimes a feeling; sometimes a story; and sometimes a blessing. She recently discovered that every painting has a song and every song has a painting.

Healing Trauma Exercise

A few gentle exercises can be completed to help heal ancestral trauma. For deeper work, it is strongly advised that you seek the help of a healer, ancestral or shamanic healer, counsellor or psychotherapist.

Ancestral Altar

Setting up an ancestral altar, for a day or longer is a powerful way of acknowledging the ancestors. This can be with using mementos with which you wish to honour the ancestral line, such as photographs. If you don't have these, you can use crystals or stones to acknowledge each ancestral line. Light a candle for each ancestral line, thanking the ancestors of that line for all their learning, while sending them love and support, and state the following prayer:

Ancestral Prayer

Before you I stand
I know I am not alone in this process
I thank you for the learning
I forgive and ask for forgiveness
It enabled me to realise who I am
The pain and the terror I release from me
To the source my highest good I turn
I call in strength, protection and positivity in my life
As I turn around, I sense a new direction has opened
A positive one and I embrace it with open arms
I stand now in my power
Moving forward into a new positive life
And so it is.

Give thanks and blow out the two candles to complete the ritual.

Forgiveness Exercise

Forgiveness is a powerful ritual, which sets you, and your ancestors free. It is a powerful gift to give yourself and your ancestors and to those people who may have caused a distortion in the ancestral field. Where there is forgiveness, there is a high concentration of unconditional source love that manifests into the ancestral fields. This energy not only is given out but it also comes back in waves. Forgiveness is the energy of unity consciousness, acknowledging the oneness in our own and other people's learning. While it can take a long time to truly forgive someone, initiating the process can lead to real liberation. Forgiveness is a way of letting go of the emotional pain connected to a hurt or abuse that occurred. When we truly forgive, we not only free ourselves from the pain and torture we have experienced. We can also liberate ancestral souls from our direct father and mother, who may be frozen in a particular aspect of time, or stuck on their soul journey due to guilt or a painful memory.

Forgiveness can be hard, but it frees the person and other soul affiliations to continue their soul journey. It is possible that if the person does not feel ready to forgive that forgiveness can be given on their behalf.

The forgiveness process should be in three parts:

1. Forgiving the person and the collective
2. Forgiving yourself
3. Forgiving yourself for any harm caused to other people.

This is a forgiveness statement. Find a quiet peaceful place to complete this process.

1. I (name) forgive say (name/group), for any hurt or trauma and for causing (state what this caused to you), in any aspect of time since the creation of my soul, past and present. I send love and healing and I let go of all negative energy attached to this experience.

2. I forgive myself for all the pain and suffering that I have experienced as a result of this experience. I let go of this negative energy from every cell of my being. I forgive myself for (state what you would like to forgive yourself for).

3. I ask forgiveness for any harm that I have caused to other people connected to this learning in past and present and for any suffering I may have caused. I set myself and other people free from this cycle of learning.

Ancestral Wisdom

Individual trauma stimulates a catalyst for change. It brings together the fragments that need to be healed. It is part of the journey. Individual trauma can push an individual to the edge of despair. Conflict aims to fragment and separate ourselves from other people, which we need to let go of. While this is not easy, this is how peace and harmony can happen. Holding the belief that there is light at the end of the tunnel and that support is there to help heal this pain, will hold a strong container for this pain to be transmuted and healed for a better life. A better life will shine a light of wisdom of all the gifts that you have to bring back to yourself. This is the alchemist journey of the soul turning lead into gold.

One of the keys to ancestral healing is not only healing the wounds from individual trauma that are connected to the past and present, but also healing the mother and father wounds from their origin. This enables the divine masculine and feminine to manifest down the ancestral lines and thus onto the planet. The manifestation of the divine masculine and feminine is the key to harmony within the self. We are all embodying the masculine and feminine energy and the wounds of both needs to be healed. Manifestation at a higher source level will lead to less individual trauma because when these are working and manifesting in harmony and balance, this delivers more of the harmonious self in all relationships.

Heart-ache is a word that draws us to the heart. What is the heart-aching for, what does it need to stop the aching and what does it need to draw to it to make us happy? The heart opens the doorways to much wisdom; it is the gateway to the source of yourself. Allow it to direct you to the change that is needed. We all deserve happiness and love and to move forward in our lives. Connect to your heart and state that you deserve immense happiness too.

The importance of manifesting the divine masculine and feminine holds the key to planetary change and more harmony on the planet. The planet can only change if the critical mass of human beings on the planet are in harmony within themselves and the earth, and from being in harmony with themselves, they create harmony on the planet.

Reflection time

*Write your insights, healing and tasks moving
forward to continue to heal your life.*

Chapter 7

Thought Forms: Driving our Reality

*Thoughts drive our reality, every twist and turn
vibrates an energy that liberates or suffocates.*

What Are Thought Forms?

Thoughts manifest our reality, and what we think also directs our behaviours and emotions. Thoughts help an individual to function in the world. They direct and transform. Thought forms are energetic patterns of emotions. We have positive and negative thought forms. They are created by our selves and some are influenced by other people. Thoughts are manifestations of what has been learnt, perceived or experienced. They contain information from our ancestors that has been hidden and contained in the shadows, concealed until the time comes to explore them. They inject an influence that it not ours, that can have negative inclinations. Before us and behind us are thoughts that hinder or empower. We are able to transform thought forms that are hindering our lives, by going to the origin of when the thought manifested.

Energy drives thoughts. Emotion is the driver that enables them to control lives. There are many thought forms, which need to be healed which is why ancestral work is so important. Thoughts are one way to expand consciousness, as well as provide access to the many stories contained within them. Our availability to connection is often limited by the restrictions we have placed on ourselves. Thoughts help provide goals as to how we can make our lives better. Thoughts can limit, and they can also aid our connection with all around us. There are thoughts within everything, and that is how creation came into being. Every aspect of creation is built of many thoughts. Good thoughts create healthy aspects of life and negative thoughts bring down the energy of creation and self.

The impact on the ancestral field is the energetic daggers that drive the negative thought form from generation to generation. This denies the individual access to their full source power. Memory exists to enable thought forms to be accessed and healed. Remembrance is all within the thought consciousness. We can connect with the negative thoughts within the field of consciousness and transmute these; all are polar opposites. There is a need to sever the ties within the energy contained within the negative thought form. It is the energy behind this, which have created the disturbances in mind and body and the conflict within the self.

Contribution to the energetic makeup of the human being is a collection of thoughts, thoughts that created DNA, our body and that which is contained within our soul. Everything has a story and thought forms behind it. When we are conscious of what is driving our behaviour, we are more likely to heal this. Being unaware of the driving force and thought behind behaviour makes it more difficult to heal.

The creation of thoughts is connected to a number of factors, including what we have chosen to experience, our past and our connection to a particular ancestor, from which this thought form originated. The aim is to track these at their origin and heal them at their core to heal the whole ancestral field of this. Practices can take place as described in this chapter, to take the emotional charge out of a thought form to heal it. The aim of Ancestral Healing Practitioners is to investigate the cause and effect of a negative thought form and to heal the thought form that no longer serves at its root. Tracking and going within the energetic structure of a thought form provides the wisdom of all that is contained within this.

Origin of Thoughts

Thoughts originate from a variety of areas, including: the source; a collective field of thought memory; our present and past timelines; and the experience of our ancestors.

Source

It is said that from a thought form, the universe was created, and so was the earth. The source is a consciousness, which contains the memory of everything and the memory of all of creation. At a higher source level, thoughts work together in harmony and balance. The source created everything as a reflection of what it is, being filled with positivity, light and love. The aim of the higher origin of thoughts at a source level was to encourage and create positive harmony and balance in the universe. The thought mind creates the original thought in the source. The source of love thoughts in their pure form are about manifesting and creating similar energy. There are golden keys within a thought which help activate a process; it unlocks doorways to create whatever the thought energy has been directed to create. This amazing matrix of information is contained within the thought form and is protected. Thoughts can also become influenced by negative forces, creating a different energy to the thought form.

Whenever we place expectations on life or self, we are going against the flow of what is right for us. Thoughts are containers of knowledge that help us to navigate our internal landscapes. The truth is within us, and we are able to dig deep enough to access it. Shining through us is an amazing consciousness that is our divine right to access. Self-gain with no regard for other people projects thoughts that attract the same. Higher source memory shows us that we are all here on earth to heal and to be in harmony with all around us.

At a source level there has always been dark or negative energies. These are manifestations of different aspects of source energy, we all learn from each other and this helps with evolution. The soul is on a journey of unconditional love and thus thoughts created from love and acting from love are a representative of what the soul is striving towards. Along the way, there are learnings in various directions that the soul goes through. The creative aspect of thoughts delves deep into consciousness. They are part of our everyday existence, and are powerful drivers of change directed to aid creation. Without thoughts, existence would not be possible. Every moment is a spark of change and thoughts help drive this. Conditioning comes from other influences that are not aligned with the divine spark in its pure intent.

Collective Thought Memory

Each experience and thought is recorded as an energetic library of information in consciousness. This serves as a way of keeping memories of thoughts, time, and information that everyone can tap into at an energetic level. Thoughts that have been created are recorded in the collective thought memory. This memory can direct what is deemed to be acceptable behaviour to achieve a result. This enables particular thought forms to be tapped into every day, along with these thought forms feeding into consciousness. This influences the behaviour of an individual; as we are automatically tapping every day into a collective memory. Negative thoughts in the collective memory can be used to control and affect other people in negative ways. This is because there is a memory of what exists; how this has affected other people; and how this has been used against other people in a negative way.

There is the collective thought form of instilling fear in other people, to control a collective of souls. These are seen in wars and in other authoritarian behaviours to control individual behaviour. This memory and thought form in the collective, continues to have an influence in feeding into the collective and influences those who see that other people can be controlled by instilling fear. Humans can use this energy of the thought memory as a means of controlling other people through fear. These memories also serve as a reminder to those who work negatively with the negative thoughts that exist to control and harm other people; and the methods that can be used to complete this.

Past and Present Timelines

Within our energetic fields are memories of thought forms that have been created from all of the soul's experiences in lifetimes of the soul's journey; nothing is lost or hidden. We have been in many different forms, both male and female and in different lands and with various experiences of, for example, wealth and status. The soul always maintains the soul story and the patterns and thoughts contained within it. The soul has a timeline, which records these experiences. It is part of the soul evolution to have contact with all the parts that are contained within it. Accessing subtle time enables access to the different periods of time, which need to be looked at.

The journey of healing can heal some of these thought forms, with the right healer and therapist. Other negative thought forms can continue to remain with the individual and continue to repeat patterns, which may hold the person back from moving forward in their lives. The soul is on a journey of harmony and balance. Therefore, negative thought forms that no longer serve us would keep repeating in lifetimes, until they are healed. These affect the soul individually and also the ancestors on an energetic level because all is connected.

Experience Ancestors

As the ancestral lineage is connected to our bloodline, many thought forms that are affecting us may have been created from the influence of ancestral patterns. There is often one particular ancestor experience, which has created this thought form down the generations. An ancestral healer can track and heal this at its origin. Negative thought forms, for example come from trauma, anger, and grief. Thought forms can amplify and manifest themselves as negative behaviours, obsessions, or addictions.

How a particular ancestral memory creates a recurring thought is a fascinating field to explore. It is connected to the learning that a particular ancestral field needs to experience and evolve through. The hardship and heartache of going through this experience can generate a number of reactions. For example, abusive behaviour towards other people, self-loathing or the creation of a gifted healer in the family who develops their gifts from healing their own wounds and helps to heal their ancestral lineage and other people's. There is a reason behind every experience of the soul. There are often repeated illnesses and behaviours that can continue down an ancestral line: for example, mental illness and drug addiction. This is because it has been passed on from generation to generation; an inheritance that does not serve the ancestor anymore at a soul level. The origin of this is often linked to a thought linked to a negative experience or trauma, which continues down the generations to create repeated behaviours or illness.

Effect of Negative Thought Forms

Effect on Self

The self is made up of a matrix of many energies. Our childhood influences, which we remember and do not remember, along with our ancestral history, can all create negative thought forms. When energies such as negative thought forms penetrate the energy field, they disperse the energetic field. This affects how we operate in the world. It could be someone who may abuse power or someone who is the victim of the abuse of power, and so the cycle continues. The memory of negative thought forms is contained within the shadow. We are often not aware of what is playing out in our own shadows. The negative and positive thoughts within ourselves often do not work in harmony and balance, and thus this infighting within the self creates disharmony.

Negative thought forms can be generated by the ego, and these can take over the personality. These thoughts can alter or cloud our perspective of a situation, which may not be necessarily true. This can cause a reaction or behaviour that is not aligned with the soul. It can hinder our lives and cause despair, repetitive patterns, and depression. A total breakdown of sanity can result in the person being unable to connect with their true self. The self moves into a perpetual cycle of behaviour that is hard to get out of which causes limitations in our lives. The ancestral field and many ancestral souls are also affected individually by these perpetual negative thought forms. These thought forms can create disease and ancestral illness that continue down the generations.

Effect on Other People

Ancestral trauma and negative thought forms can be said to have created much of the trauma in the world towards other people. Thoughts are often subtle, but they are very powerful. Of course, positive thoughts create positive lives for the individual and those people around them. Thoughts do not circulate on their own; they are directed like crossfire in battle when directed negatively to other people. They gain pace depending on how much passion is behind them to direct them. It is a chain reaction to other people that this thought form creates. The effect on other people can be harmful and in turn the affected individual creates negative thought forms and affects other people. For example, an alcoholic father and the behaviour generated by this addiction can sometimes influence his children into following similar addictive behaviour. The effect of this on the consciousness and on the ancestors is huge. Therefore, negative thought forms are an important energy to heal. On mass this energy feeds into consciousness and moves away from unity and harmony. Individuals and collectives of individuals embodying the energy of negative thoughts pass them down the generations. This can form repeated patterns in behaviours towards other people. An individual may not often be aware of the negative thought form that is playing out and the effect this has on other people.

Negative thought forms impact on a number of areas of life, for example, on relationships. The thought form of not being good enough, could affect the dynamic in relationships of constantly having feelings of jealousy. This creates a ripple effect on behaviour. For example, a man from a violent background who has experienced violence from his father, whose father had also had the same experience, could manifest the thought forms of violence and anger towards other people and continue this behaviour.

Spiritual Attachment/Possession

Negative thought forms can weaken the energetic field because they are not aligned with the source consciousness of the energy field, making a person vulnerable to a spiritual attachment. A spiritual attachment can be, for example, an earthbound spirit, who attaches to a weak energy field.

When the energy field is scattered or weakened, protection can also be weakened, creating gaps and weaknesses that make it easier for other energies to attach themselves to the person. These attachments can make it harder for the person to move out of these negative thought forms. They can affect the individual in a number of ways, for example increasing tiredness and weakening the spirit. These spirits can feed in negative thought forms to that person. These negative thought forms are not in resonance with the personality of the person and so the cycle continues. Curses can be made by sending a negative thought form via an element to the person; thus it is the power of the thought forms in manifesting reality.

Energetic Structure of a Thought Form

A thought form has an energetic structure; it is a powerful energy form that creates and destructs. Thoughts are very important because they enable the individual to live in the human world. Positive thoughts are powerful drivers for engineering positive change in a person's life. We need thought forms to live and to create our reality, but it is the negative aspects that we need to heal and transform to create a better life. Understanding the origin of thoughts, allows an awareness that can heal.

The diagram below shows the structure of a thought form. Going around in a clockwise rotation, moving from: influence to timeframe; to emotion and behaviour attached, provides a dynamic structure to investigate and heal thought forms.

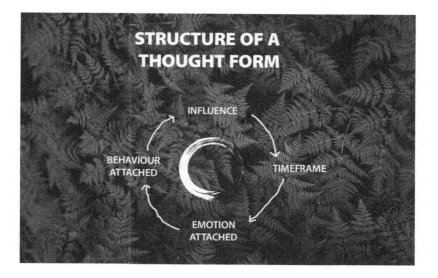

Influence

Thought forms have an influence; it is the influence that created them, whether this was ancestors, peers, or other influences. Feeding into consciousness are also the collective thought forms that can engineer and influence individual behaviour. There are many influences from other people, which are a constant in daily life, along with the influence of what has occurred in the past in the ancestral field. The influences that create a negative thought form are often linked to trauma and the connection to the person or groups who created it.

Ancestral Story
Wanting to be superior to other people

Prior to the thought form healing session Joanna observed thought patterns within herself and identified a core thought form that was not serving her, which was in need of healing. She observed this carefully and began to understand its temperament. She saw how the thought form was leading her to believe that, 'I must achieve more than other people, be better than other people and I am in competition with other people'. This thought form was characterised by an internal judgemental attitude enabling her to constantly compare herself to other people. This was her search for acceptance and developing an egoistic desire to be superior. The thought form created a sense of inequality and separation.

The thought form had started when she was a young teen. It was a time when Joanna learned from her environment that she had a different ethnicity to the majority of the people around her. This gave her a feeling that she was different and she struggled to identify with other people. At this age, she also discovered society's hierarchical class system and again she could not identify herself with any one level. The thought form began to develop as a coping strategy for being in society.

The emotions associated with this thought form were anxiety, nervousness, frustration, annoyance, self-doubt, jealousy and anger, all working together to result in low self-esteem. These emotions also affected Joanna's physical body by causing tension and shallow breathing and created a negative set of behaviours. This led her to speak in a short, aggressive and hasty tone, releasing her inner frustrations on to other people. It also caused her to behave in inauthentic ways by looking outside of herself for validation and trying to fit in. The other behaviour she exhibited was being over-talkative out of nervousness and a desire to show her knowledge, again in search of external validation. Jealousy and low self-esteem obstructed her ability to develop true relationships.

The ancestral healer journeyed to find the origin of this thought form. It was discovered that Joanna had a female ancestor who once was an alchemist working with symbols and potions. She was not fully understood by her community and was chosen to be sacrificed to death. She was hanged and her last moments in that life was feeling the tightness of the rope around her neck and looking back at a crowd of people all chanting for her to die. It appeared that she had been chosen to be hanged by the crowd and she could not understand why. She did not want to die, but felt she had no choice. As a result of this, anger, frustration, and a lack of acceptance were her last emotions, creating the thought forms of these emotions. The shamanic divination showed how this story had been carried through her mother's side, down through the entire female lineage until it could be stopped and healed by transcending it with love. The client also saw through her own shamanic journeying that this thought form was being carried down the female generation, generation after generation and that she could clear it now and stop future generations from connecting with similar thought forms.

This thought form was healed by drumming around her and sending love frequencies straight into her heart. Joanna said she felt herself drop into her heart space. The drumming also cleared the thought form from her head. During the healing process she felt more clarity in her mind and warmth in her heart. After the shamanic drumming, she said a forgiveness statement to her ancestors and forgave herself for the behaviours she had

*enacted that may have affected other people and herself.
She saw a vision of the thought form as a cloud lifting
out of her head.*

*Following this healing, Joanna said she felt a shift within,
a sense of openness, peace and oneness. During the night
of the healing she practised yoga and felt more space had
opened in her body. She felt in tune and alignment with her
body. She heard her body telling her exactly how to move
and stretch, as if her senses were heightened. She says she
continues to feel this connection in her yoga practice and
her body feels amazing and she feels much more clarity.
She is now able to observe her thought patterns more
easily and any negative thought forms that do arise she
lets them float away. She now has more distance between
herself and the negative thought forms she felt before the
healing. She used to be more consumed by them, thinking
they were a constant part of her. This healing helped her
gain more clarity day by day. She is in more in control of
her behaviours and is consciously making choices in the
present moment rather than from unhealthy patterns. By
seeing the thought form Joanna can now transcend these
by creating positive thought forms and as she described,
"I let go of the need for external validation because I am
already whole in myself".*

Timeframe

Tracking the time when a thought form that needs to be healed originated is the key to healing it; helping the past and the future. What was the timeframe when this was created? Where in subtle time, past or present? Subtle time refers to the energy of time, which exists simultaneously, i.e. past, present, and future at the same time. A person can often identify where in their present life a particular thought manifested. It is those from past lives or connected to ancestors, which require further investigation. From shamanic journeying into the subtle timeline the origin of a problem is identified. Thoughts begin their journey somewhere and they have a journey of completion at a particular time. We are able to transcend thoughts that are not serving us anymore. Navigation of time gives us an opportunity to heal and transform. Thoughts and consciousness like any energy evolve to a higher vibrational form during time, like all evolutionary journeys.

A time guardian, who is a guardian of a soul timeline, oversees the navigation of the timeline. To help with healing, the healer will need to have access to the soul timeline via the time guardian. What is held in our soul's timeline is sacred and healing is a sacred act that requires access to heal.

Emotion Attached

What is the emotion attached to the thought form? How does the person feel when they think about the thought form? The author Ian Glynn, in his book, *An Anatomy of Thought*, describes emotions as: "Emotions as distinct from moods are generally about something, a loss, a success, a danger, an obstacle, a person" There are also normally bodily changes in relation to an emotion when it needs to be expressed.

Emotions contain years of conditioning, from our childhoods, past lives, and from our ancestral lineage. Triggers or remembrance connected to a particular emotion can result in the expression of emotion in particular ways. The way the body responds to emotion is involuntary. This can result in various bodily actions, such as nausea, anxiety and anger. Emotions are connected to events or something that has occurred, for example, a death, or the ending of a relationship. In the ancestral field an emotional response could be related to something that has occurred in the ancestral field, and this emotion is contained within the individual's energetic field. Emotion manifests in the physical body, for example in relation to the amygdala, this is a set of neurons, in an almond-shape located deep in the brain's medial temporal lobe. This is shown to play a key role in not only handling current stimuli with emotional content, but it also plays a central role in emotional memory. These emotions can create illness, which can continue down the ancestral line.

Ancestral Story
Constantly judging oneself and other people

Eliza felt she was constantly being judged. This thought form created the need to judge herself and other people and everything she or other people did constantly. It was because of a fear of judgement from other people that she limited her expression and did not put herself fully out there in the world. Fear of judgement caused her feelings of embarrassment and being laughed at, exacerbating feelings of abandonment and loneliness. Ultimately, this thought form was feeding from a fear of being alone. The influence of this thought form was creating separation from her living in the world. This was related to not living her truth. This made her suffer and feel depressed and anxious when expression was not allowed to happen freely. There was also anxiety from the constant judgements, which made her life very difficult.

What influenced this was shame from being criticised by her parents for expressing her feelings or getting upset. Eliza had constant memories of her parents arguing and yelling in a car at each other and telling her not to yell out ever. This created thought forms of unfairness. She felt judged by her parents and that she was not good enough for them and therefore would not be enough for other people. To try and deal with this, she felt she should change or she should be different so she would be loved more and be happier and maybe not so alone. She wanted to be different and constantly looking for validation from her parents, especially for her father's acceptance. With this thought form she was not able to gain acceptance for herself. She had experienced these thought forms since the age of four or five.

The emotions attached to these thought forms were: the shame of being criticised; the guilt of being who she was and not being someone else who was better; the fear of being embarrassed; fear of abandonment; anxiety; and self-hatred. The negative behaviour that was expressed was mistrust towards other people and mistrust of self. She had feelings that she always had to watch her back and be concerned about what other people thought about her and being able to be vulnerable and open. Her daily expression of this was being cold and closed towards other people and not sharing herself and her vision honestly and hating herself for it. There were problems with having real relationships and committing to them because she had constant feelings of wanting to give up and move on due to a fear of being judged.

During shamanic journeying the origin of the thought form was discovered in a past life when she was as a shaman in a cave casting spells into the fire. Behind her back a void opened; she was holding her back against the void and covering it up at the same time. Eliza was forging a large iron axe, which was creating protection for her like Thor's Hammer. The journey highlighted the feelings of vulnerability she was experiencing in this lifetime. Healing was sent to heal this lifetime of these feelings. She visited the memory of her parents when they told her not to express herself. She imagined herself telling them what they had transferred to her. She explained that she would no longer carry it, it was unfair and she had suffered long enough. This changed the memory of being judged and the memory of not speaking her truth. The shamanic journey returned the negative thought forms to their origins, with gratefulness and forgiveness. Rattling was also completed for healing and help from animal guides was given.

After the healing Eliza focused on being kinder to herself and let go of the self-hatred and judgement and focused on forgiving her parents. She started to take conscious steps towards trusting other people more and opening up and challenging her negative thought forms and actively paying attention to bring love towards her. Changes in her personal relationships have been transformational since she started to work with her thought forms. She felt that this type of approach to healing was a great tool to help people towards self-realisation and to bring opportunities to bring a 'death' to the old self and to give up what does not serve anymore.

Behaviour Attached

There always appears to be a behavioural response as an outlet for reacting with what has been experienced and the effect this has had. Negativity creates behaviours that do not serve the individual or those people around them. Throughout history, the ancestors have experienced traumatic behaviour towards them creating negative thought forms and behaviour towards other people and towards themselves. Negative thought forms can also be internalised and so behaviour is turned on the self, or externalised and directed to other people.

The behaviours a person exhibits as a result of negative thought forms can vary. These can be expressions of anger, isolation, narcissistic behaviour, and various other behaviours. This is often detrimental to themselves and those people around them. Behaviour is often the way that a negative thought forms manifests and shows itself externally.

Ancestral Story
Other people put me in danger

Rob focused on a thought form entitled: 'Other people can put me in danger'. He felt this affected his life and it could be traced to his father's ancestral line.

A shamanic divination was completed. Rob was asked what the thought form was and the timeframe in which he felt it had affected him, the emotion it caused him to feel and how it had impacted on his behaviour. He described how this had affected him since childhood; perhaps between the ages of 5-10 and that it made him feel fearful and caused him to behave awkwardly or timidly sometimes. It was explained to Rob that the ancestors connected to his father's line would be able to assist in the healing process. The ancestral healer evoked the energetic hut around them both and used a rattle to go into a trance. Rob meditated and focused on accepting healing. The Ancestral healer told him that she saw a vision of an eagle and a lion and an ancestor who feared greatly the concept of 'power' as well as the idea of losing power. These thought forms about the fear of power continued down the generations. The ancestral healer sent healing to this ancestor and she went on to use her rattle to send healing energy to his heart. She had a vision of Rob wearing a grey coat and when instructed he opened the coat with his mind's eye revealing a body of gold shimmering light inside. He was advised to research the shamanic symbolism of the two animals represented, the eagle and the lion, and he was told his spiritual team strongly protected him.

After the healing process, Rob said he felt that he was allowed to fully detach from this thought form. However, shortly after this healing an altercation manifested between himself and a stranger, in which the thought form of 'other people can put me in danger' began to arise. In the light of the recent healing he had received, the thought form was not able to take hold and instead a more positive thought form came into his awareness, which repeated in his mind; "I am always protected". This led to a smooth unfolding of events during the alteration, which neutralised tension instead of accelerating it. The client had passed the universal test, which presented itself after his healing.

Healing Thought Forms Exercise

This powerful exercise enables you to delve deep into the thought form that is affecting you, and to heal the aspects contained within this. This can raise awareness of the origin of the thought form. Being aware of the origin of the thought form is very healing in itself.

Create a safe meditation space in a quiet space, where you are not disturbed. Write down the negative thought forms which have been having an adverse impact on your life. Connect to silence and be aware of what thoughts come through as you connect with and receive general information on each thought form and how you can heal and transform these.

Connect to the diagram on the energetic structure of thought forms on page 169 and for each thought form go to each of the elements within it and ask for guidance on each area. For example, concentrating on one thought form you would look at: what was the influence that created the negative thought form? Work through the diagram of the energetic makeup of a thought form, moving around this in a clockwise direction. Make note of the following aspects listed below.

1. Influences: What are the circumstances/influences that may have caused this?
2. Timeframe: How long have you had these feelings/thoughts?
3. Emotions: What emotions are attached to these thought forms?
4. Behaviours: What negative behaviours do you feel are being expressed as the result of this?

The key is to go to the core emotion you or the person you are working with is experiencing, as a result of the thought form, for example, anger. Be aware of this emotion, bring this to the heart and breathe into the heart asking for this to be healed and transformed. You can do this in your mind's eye by asking for healing to be sent, or if working with someone, using a rattle or hands-on healing to help the healing of the emotion to take place. Complete a forgiveness process if appropriate, to those people who created these thought forms that affected you and your ancestors. Please note, even if you are not aware of the origin of this, this process will provide great healing and transformation.

Also, state the following.

I return this thought form to its origin

I illuminate it with love

I am grateful for the learning

I ask forgiveness of all soul affiliations who I may have harmed by creating this, and forgive all those people who have created this and who may have caused me harm

I set myself free from the influence of this thought form forever, so I can move forward in my life.

Ancestral Wisdom

Thoughts are powerful energies and are drivers for particular behaviour. Being aware of our thoughts and the connection to the origin of negative thoughts in the ancestral field, leads to healing and transformation for our ancestors and ourselves. Moving through step-by-step into the energetic makeup of the thought form and looking at and healing the different aspects, transforms and heals. Reflect on the self and your thoughts, and the thoughts which have been negative and have impacted negatively on your life. Tracking the origin of these, increases awareness and healing. When we heal these we also contribute to the healing of the collective as the thought form contains many stories of a thought form repeating down the generations.

We can also connect to the thoughts that have been jumbled in our minds and disentangling those that are limiting. Thoughts need to be in harmony with each other, so we can be in harmony with ourselves. Information, which manifests into matter, is created by our own thoughts and feelings and they can often limit our behaviour and social engagements with other people.

Healing the thoughts unlocks the wisdom within which may have been weighed down by the restricted thought. Part of the locking down process is to disconnect the person from their true source power. This may have been negotiated and arranged by the soul, as part of their learning and evolution. There is always a potential for this to be changed during the lifetime of the soul, but it is an opportunity that not everyone embraces; change can be frightening for some people, the status quo feels safer.

Negative thought forms are powerful energies, which can form destructive behaviour for the individual and other people. When we heal, we help the ancestors who have been affected by them and we help the future generations. Love and harmony are about balance, and negative thought forms cause humanity to be out of balance. They no longer serve the self or humanity and this is an aspect of our ancestral inheritance we can heal and transform.

Imagine a path that is showing no end, there is a tree and another path, a sign that there is something different that changes how the path appears. Changing a thought allows a different view to be taken of a behaviour or pattern and shows a different path, one that is less barren and full of life of growth and development filled with joy.

Reflection time

*Write your insights, healing and tasks moving
forward to continue to heal your life.*

Chapter 8

Ancestral Illness: Wounds of the Past

Illness is a great teacher, the journey to wellness can bring awareness of ancestor stories of the past affecting the present.

Illness Through the Generations

When we are born, we take on the history of our ancestors. We inherently carry some of the ancestral baggage with us, including the predisposition to certain illness. They are not always created from present life experiences, but from experiences that have gone before. The energetic make up of illness contains stories of experiences that manifested this into reality. There are many compartments that can be opened to reveal the origin of the problem and the reasons why the illness keeps being repeated through the generations. The challenges we choose at a soul level are to heighten our awareness for our own learning, along with an opportunity for healing deep, repetitive issues. Sometimes illness is chosen as our chosen time to die. It is easy to blame the mother or father line for our issues, but delving deeper reveals the ancestral stories that hold the keys to ancestral illness. This started in the ancestral field, way before the mother and father in the present time reality. The soul has a programme, which can manifest an illness in the lifetime that the soul chose; the accumulation of ancestral and individual circumstances. During the current important time on the planet, many souls have chosen to carry the immense burden of the ancestral karma on behalf of the ancestors to help clear patterns that no longer serve, contributing to both the ancestral and planetary evolution.

To heal an illness, it is important to know the inherent combination of factors that created the illness in the first place. There is a need to navigate to the origin, whether this is from the mother or father line and where the distortion in the energy field originated. Ancestral illness is there to connect people to their roots of connection and remembering some of the ancestral stories that lead to the ancestral you. There is the possibility of remembering the story that created the illness and the possibility of healing the illness within the self and the ancestral collective.

When we are navigating the ancestral fields and searching for the origin of illness, we are entering into a field of energy, which could hold the secrets to genetic evolution. There is individual ancestral history to the origin of the problem and beyond that the collective source origin. This filters into the collective and contributes to the creation of illness in the ancestral field in the first place. Memory in the collective exists in order for access to be gained to memories that are there for our learning and evolution.

When we identify with an ancestral illness that repeats down through the generations, we are identifying with ourselves. It is challenging having an ancestral illness, which is inherited, and the stigma that goes with this. However, exploring energetically the story behind this paves the way for peace and transformation and healing, and eliminates the propensity to this illness in the future. Illness takes the person on a journey, which provides signposts for those who are open to awareness of the components that manifested all the memories of trauma and karmic factors into the physical body. The body becomes in disharmony and malfunctions with the manifestation of illness. The body aims to adapt to all that is contained within the energy of the shadow, which the body has chosen to manifest at a particular time.

Indigenous Wisdom

Indigenous people throughout the world have held and hold inherent knowledge and wisdom about illness and how it can be healed. In some African traditions, a person who is undergoing spiritual, emotional, and mental distress is seen as their ancestors as communicating a call to be a Sangoma, a traditional healer. Often this call is misunderstood, and the person is left with their illness and unsupported on their path to be a healer.

In the Zulu tradition, when people discuss misfortune and disease, it can be linked to ancestral spirits. It can be related to an ancestor who is angry and if they are offended, they can come down hard on the living ancestor. David Bogopa, in his article, "The Case of South Africa and Beyond", discusses the Tswana speaking urbanites using the categories of illness as deemed to be: "As a result of sorcery, natural illness, and illness caused by the ancestors. Illnesses, which are believed to have been caused by ancestors including, among many others: strokes, mumps, leprosy, and vitiligo."

In some traditional healing methods in Africa, a drumming ceremony is held for the person who needs to be healed. The patient who needs healing will walk or dance around in a circle, which often creates a trance like state. The patient usually collapses on the floor and while the person is in this state, the traditional healer will listen to what the person has to say. The spirits will speak through the patient, while the patient is in this state. The traditional healer will listen to the ancestors communicating through the patient as to the cause of the illness and provide the appropriate healing.

Traditional healers can perceive illness as an evil that has been added to the body. The aim of the traditional healer is also to diagnose the cause of the illness and implement the appropriate treatment. Many traditional healers work with ancestral spirits to complete healing particularly in South Africa. An interesting concept is from the Ngoma tradition of healers. They consider that when a client is unwell, this stems from a pattern in the human relationship. The author John Janzen in his book, *Ngoma*, explains that the healer goes into possession and the individual is encouraged to create a healing song of their own. The healing song sang by the individual helps to aid the healing process.

The author Victor W Turner in his book, *The Ritual Process*, describes that according to the Ndembu tradition, all persistent or severe sickness, is believed to be caused by the: "Punitive action of ancestral shades, or by the secret malevolence of male sorcerers or female witches." He describes that the cure of this is divination to find the origin of the problem, this illuminates any struggles between an individual and factions. Indigenous cultures have much to teach us regarding how illness has an origin that can be tracked in the ancestral fields or to a situation, which created the problem in the first place.

Origin of Ancestral Illness

Ancestral illness has an origin, which comes from various planes of existence. What humanity creates, feeds into different levels of consciousness which has a reciprocal effect of recycling this into consciousness. It moves within and is contained within the source collective and ancestral collective. This causes a distortion in the DNA, which manifests in a spirit of illness and consequently as an illness in the body.

Source Collective

Within the source collective are memories of everything that has existed in the universe. It provides records of information many of which can be accessed. There are of course negative and positive energies and memories that are contained within this. This can include memories of individual and collective trauma and of fear and abuse; these have an influence and feed into consciousness. Ancestors have a great influence on other people and this can create ways to either enhance other people or work to their detriment.

The source collective is a place where everything meets and is stored in the cellular memory; it feeds in and it influences. Information can be extracted out and information put in. There is a cosmic dance with all that has been before interweaving and being placed in its appropriate compartment until the box is accessed or opened. There are the appropriate guardians of specific information. There are also free flowing information energies and thoughts, which have an influence on those who connect with this.

All this information feeds into the ancestral collective that is connected to a particular energy type or memory. The ancestral field is a collective, holding collective memory. There can be positive gifts of the ancestors, along with the negative ones. The light and the dark are always in place. The aims of both differ, but they each have a role in shifting consciousness in one way or another, this also supports and directs consciousness. Within our own ancestral fields are different resonances of soul vibrations. We are free to be influenced by souls in the ancestral field. However, the soul usually connects more with those souls in similar resonance and frequency.

Ancestral Collective

The ancestral collectives have different soul frequencies but are connected by common ancestors. They are holders of positive and negative energies. When healing is sent into the generations of ancestors, it enables the release of old patterns and behaviours that are manifesting in the form of illness. The drawing board of a particular ancestral collective draws out the wounds and the common repeating wounds. They repeat because they need to be freed and healed, so thousands of souls can heal that aspect of themselves. Ancestral connection serves or dominates, two different energies serving this connection.

There are souls in the ancestral field of connection who are happy to serve to heal connections and other souls who wish to hinder evolution. Souls are also on their own process, while allowing the unhealthy patterns which are creating illness to be freed from others. There are gatekeepers of these ancestral tribes who step forward to help the transmissions of healing to move down the generations, healing thousands of souls at the same time. The memory and healing of the ancestral collective is extremely important because it holds the memories of thousands of ancestors. This includes the positive gifts that can be offered to the ancestors, along with awareness of the pain that has continued down the generations resulting in similar patterns.

The ancestors are able with the help of others to uncover this information, which is needed to find the origin of the problem and the illness. They wait in anticipation for an ancestor who has been chosen to carry this burden on their back, to heal or seek healing, to liberate this aspect from the ancestral field and create healing. The ancestral collective field can often be disjointed and entangled with broken lines, which have created a disconnection. All the souls are connected by their ancestry but they are also individual souls with individual journeys. There are aspects of their souls embedded with the ancestors. Soul evolution is about healing them which automatically heals the collective connected to a particular trauma, which can be thousands of ancestors.

We are in a cosmic song together and together we dance in the universe, which is held in the heart of one connection. We may try to run from this connection, but it will always find us. It is in our blood and our bones, our hearts and our minds, a burden and a gift, a chance to make real change. The ancestors may be understood as archetypal representations of the collective unconscious, and all we need is the opportunity to become the translation of our lives. The ancestor stories help us to translate the cause and origin of illness, which we have embodied. One simple act of connecting to the origin and healing this for ourselves can transform thousands of ancestor's lives and impact on the collective shift in consciousness.

Ancestral Story
Alcoholism

An ancestral healer worked with John to help him to heal issues connected to having a mum who was an alcoholic. Her condition had affected John in many ways and he suffered from low self-esteem. During the investigations into the ancestral fields, she discovered that this story was connected to John's grandmother who had a bad temper and strong energy. Divination discovered that centuries ago, an ancestor, a young girl witnessed a horrible crime towards her family. This child in her anger at the people who had committed the crime, turned to black magic and caused harm to other people who were involved. This anger and energy carried on through the generations. Unfortunately, John's grandmother carried this energy and passed this to John's mother, the effect of which was that John's mother carried the energy of this curse and entities, and became addicted to alcohol.

The ancestral healer helped to facilitate a process of forgiveness; to forgive those people who had been involved in the crime, which had caused a distortion in the ancestral field, while also seeking forgiveness from those people who had been affected. The curse and the entities attached to the curse were also removed. John felt better in his everyday life and he felt more able to move forward with positivity.

DNA and Epigenics

DNA is the abbreviation for deoxyribonucleic acid. This is the molecule that contains the genetic code of organisms. Chromosomes are inherited from our parents. One chromosome from each of your 23 pairs came from each of your parents. The two chromosomes of a pair (except for the sex chromosomes) contain the same genes, but the genes have small differences.

Illness is created from a distorted field of energy, which consequently has an effect on genes through the generations. Distortions cause our energy fields not to be aligned which affects the energy expression of our whole being. Energy expression has a connection to DNA. It is acknowledged by studies in epigenetics that environmental and circumstances in life affect the genes. They can be silenced or turned off, become dormant, or turned on again and become active.

The human script is made to function in a harmonious world; it was designed that way, a formula for the harmonious man. The script, which we call DNA, reacts and shifts against the disharmonious form. The disharmonious form is created by trauma and behaviour that inflicts trauma on other people. Humans have often created their own illnesses by being disjointed and disconnected from their true essence. The ancestral illness creates a distortion in the DNA, which continues down the generations. DNA helps code the human body and the codes are transmitted in complex ways, with information that has gone before. This helps shape the individual; it is a transmission of information.

Epigenetics is the study of biological mechanisms that will switch genes on and off. It is believed that genes were no longer thought to be acting independently, but rather in constant interaction with each other and one way in which genetic regions can maintain a memory, even after a stimulus has gone. This means that our genes remember the initial stimulus if that stimulus returns again, for example the memory of a collective trauma because this is stored the gene memory. Researchers have discovered that the descendants of holocaust survivors have lower levels of the hormone cortisol, which helps their body bounce back after trauma. This suggests there has been a change in an aspect of gene behaviour to create this.

We now know that all human races have the same genes but how they differ is that each gene comes in alternative forms, which geneticists know as alleles. For many years, scientists writing about genetics, wrote about them as if they were fixed and they could not be changed. However, there is exciting research in recent years showing that the environment also has an influence on gene expression. Epigenetics discuss that gene expression on one generation will influence and affect the gene expression in the next few generations. We know that collective trauma throughout the generations has a direct impact on the ancestral lineage and the patterns, behaviour and illnesses that manifest. The ancestors are part of our bloodline and we cannot but be influenced by what they have experienced before, for good and bad.

Ancestral Story
Parkinson's disease

Sonia wanted to heal Parkinson's disease in the family connected to her mother's side. Divination by the ancestral healer revealed distortion originated from an ancestral issue of trauma. A young male ancestor was with his younger brother and other village children in Africa. They were playing and walking through the jungle and forest and came across a snake pit in a clearing in the woods, which showed snakes covering the floor. Her ancestor was aware of danger and that they were in an area they should not be. His younger brother who was playful and a risk taker, decided to skip over the snakes and run across the snake pit. The other children were aware of danger and were fearful. He tried to tell his brother to stop and stay away from the snakes but he was too busy showing off. The brother was bitten by a snake and fell to the ground poisoned by a neuron toxin. He was convulsing and repeatedly bitten. He had a painful gruesome death, watched by the ancestor and other village children.

Observing the shocking death scene and the loss of his brother and the feeling of responsibility for the event, the ancestor was immediately physically and emotionally traumatised. He began to shake and shudder and wail, and could not speak and was in severe physical and emotional pain. The village children and the other village members were frightened and lacked understanding of how the trauma was manifesting in the ancestor. They became suspicious and fearful. They interpreted his traumatic response as mimicking the effect of the neuron toxin that killed his brother.

They believed he was carrying the spirit of the snake that had killed his brother. From that day they treated him with suspicion, he was ostracised and there were repeated attempts to exorcise him causing further trauma and symptoms. Sonia's ancestor became emotionally suppressed and unable to adapt to his life and move on. He was disconnected from his mind, body, and soul.

While the ancestral healer was working, she could see a black snake present behind her client and saw ancestors also wearing black snakes. The ancestral healer embarked on a shamanic journey to connect with the spirit of illness and was shown the heart. The origin was with the heart, heartbroken, heart wound and heart loss, there was grief for the loss of a child. The heart was squeezed, compressed and ravaged by broken shards of glass. This heart pain was too hard to bear, therefore causing a total shut down of the body and mind and disconnection from life and body. This was an attempt to protect from the

*pain of life. Life force, joy, and happiness was drained
from the body and life became grey and monotone.*

*With guidance the ancestral healer felt that the
ancestor needed colour to transform and heal, like a
blood transfusion, but with colour. She needed also to
remove heart shards and also to give heart healing and
integration of the heart, body, and mind. On behalf of the
ancestor she sent healing to realign his body and spirit.
This healed the broken heart of the ancestor who suffered
death by the snake, to allow his spirit to go to the light.
She also sent healing to remove the energy of the snake
that caused the ancestral illness of Parkinson's disease. At
the same time healing was given to the ancestor who felt
ostracised and responsible for his brother's death. This
aspect of the session was completed, by sending healing
to realign the client to heal mind, body, and spirit and to
heal the broken heart.*

*Removing the energy of the snake was more complex
and took three stages. Firstly, the ancestral healer
reduced its size with a rattle and help from the spiritual
guides. Secondly, a path was cleared through the forest
and the snake taken to the light by a guide. Thirdly, the
snake was observed as gone from the client's aura, but its
presence was still felt. The healer saw a black line behind
her client, which was separate from her. She tuned in
and felt the snake was clear from her client, but not from
ancestral line.*

*The healer had to bring energy in to clear the snake
from the ancestral line. Healing was given to the brain
and spinal column for integration. The heart shards
were removed and the colour gold transmitted to the
solar plexus. A space was created for the merging with
the lion for future strength, to be able to deal with
life and situations. A light ball manifested above the*

client's head, so light would lead the way for her path. Finally, a transmission to help reconfigure, harmonise, and balance the DNA in relation to abandonment and loneliness was given by the healer and the session was concluded. The client felt it was a very powerful session and that their work had been completed to clear this from the ancestral field.

Spirit of Illness

This energy relates to the ancestral soul memory and individual soul memory. It is a very powerful energy and needs to be connected to with respect. It is the essence of what is playing out in the ancestral illness and this spirit can operate in unusual ways. Where there is an illness, there is a spirit. The spirit of illness is waiting to be seen and heard. The spirit is a manifestation of the memory of the energy of the spirit of an illness. It is the carrier of energy that passes the illness from generation to generation. This spirit can be thousands of years old, depending on when the problem originated.

The spirit of illness can show itself in various ways. It can show itself in an energy form, human form, and animal form. From being able to communicate with the spirit of illness, information on the origin of the illness and what can be done to cure the illness is received. The spirit of illness is a powerful force of energy. Attached to this also could be entities that try to sabotage communication, or present hurdles that need to be overcome. The spirit of illness is a container of knowledge that is not easy to access because it is so important in the healing process. Complex stories are often heard from the spirit of illness, which are connected to the individual and the ancestors. It is embedded in the soul and provides a way of understanding an illness.

The spirit embodies the illness and translates the story behind the scenes of what is hidden. It accumulates the collective song that cries out to be healed. The lessons and learnings are contained within the spirit of illness all have to be looked at and harmonised. The outcome is the successful healing of the energetic distortion, which caused ancestral illness that travels through time.

Body

The ancestral illness manifests in the body at a time when there may be an emotional trigger, or when the soul chooses for its soul learning. Symptoms and going through an illness are not easy but from this process comes the ability to be able to accumulate insights and bring a focus to the matter. The illness works its way through the system and through a process of pain. The pain showing the holding of a memory that at some stage has created a painful existence. Contrary to belief, illness is a contributory factor in the translation of every memory in history because similar diseases are created from aspects of similar history. These aspects come together to create an illness that mirrors the different aspects of stories of experience, which are similar between individuals. Our consciousness and souls often need to experience the pain of being embodied on Earth, which has created so many humanitarian memories, memories made by our ancestors before us. The burden of truth is within us all and the truth can be of a perpetrator and a victim. Memory is stored in our cells. Each cell has its particular memory, which records and remembers. We can remember pain and remember how to heal that pain. Illness needs to be viewed with respect because it operates according to time, matter, and body, matter being where the person has chosen to incarnate. Time is regulated by the soul at the start of the journey. All aspects of the journey are within a particular time consortium, for time periods of learning and challenges.

Illness in the body is a programme that enables the human to experience. The pain of the ancestors in one way or another translates the story that unfolds and so does the different strands that come together to track the parts that need to be healed. Going through the process of healing from an illness, can make a person feel more empowered to move to another level of their soul evolution. This empowerment, connected to ancestors, also ripples down through the generations.

Energetic Makeup of Ancestral Illness

There are various factors that feed into the ancestral field which contributes towards ancestral illness that continues down through generations. When illness manifests, the origin of this lies in the ancestral field. The energetic makeup of an illness can consist of one or a combination of factors as outlined in the diagram. Illness is a complex weave of various factors. To cure illness, the factors that are contributing to the illness need to be delved into, treated and healed one by one.

For example, a collective ancestral trauma could result in a weakened energy field, resulting in entities being attached to the person, along with negative thought forms from the experience. This can be passed down through the generations and shows itself in the manifestation of illness.

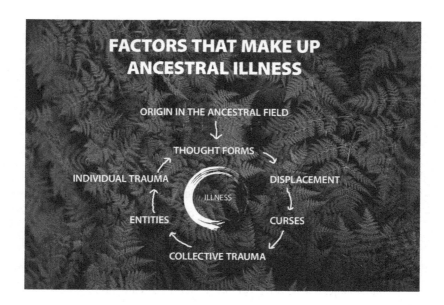

FACTORS THAT MAKE UP ANCESTRAL ILLNESS

ORIGIN IN THE ANCESTRAL FIELD

THOUGHT FORMS

INDIVIDUAL TRAUMA

DISPLACEMENT

ILLNESS

ENTITIES

CURSES

COLLECTIVE TRAUMA

When we are able to see into the energetic makeup of an illness, we are able to go into all the various areas to heal it. The diagram above outlines some of the factors that make up illness. The healer will need to track where it started and heal and deal with all the elements that need to be healed within the illness matrix.

Ancestral Story
Anxiety disorder

Joan came to the ancestral healer for support with her anxiety disorder, which she had since she was six years old. She observed that both her father and mother had personal experiences of anxiety, in particular her father who she felt had greater symptoms.

The healer completed divination to gain insight into the origin of Joan's anxiety disorder, where the illness came from and which ancestral line it belonged to. Secondly, the divination was conducted to connect to the spirit of the illness to see how it could be transformed. The ancestral healer worked with her spirit guides and asked to be shown insights and to be given messages to convey to Joan.

The knowledge that she gained from the first divination was that the illness originated in 1880. The illness came from the mother's ancestral line and had the texture of thick blood, really dense, strong, and tangible. She was also shown the vision of a creature that had a thick tar textured body. This creature was a powerful spirit, not from the earth, trapped on the earth and invisible to the naked eye. It was the spores that it emitted which created the anxiety disorder due to its distressed state, which was received by an ancestor in its vicinity.

The healer was also shown a vision of an ancestor of Joan, on her mother's side, a great-uncle who was a spiritual man belonging to a male cult in southern Europe. This cult had a sunroom made of sand stone with open slits for windows. At the top of the room to let the golden sunlight in, Joan's ancestor had created a positive energy centre. Within this was a large flat yellow-golden orange disc on top of a table, where a person could place an arm, hand or head to be healed. The healer's guide said that Joan should meditate energetically in this place and use it as an energy source to help her. Her guide also said that it would be good for Joan to take away with her the energy of this place and her ancestors in her heart.

Another divination was completed to see how the spirit of this illness could be transformed. The healer journeyed to the lower world and was taken to a waterfall made of golden lava. She was told that the solution was to reach the bottom of the waterfall. She was shown there were three ways to do so. The first was the most painful and it involved being impaled on a giant tree and sliding down. The second was gentler because it involved simply climbing down a ladder made of wood attached to the rock face and the third was on the back of her spirit animal. The ancestral healer decided to take the third option. When they arrived at the bottom, there was a dusty forest clearing and her spirit guide was there. The waterfall fell away and manifested into a pool of golden lava. The waterfall formed two spiralling whirlpools and in that pool the healer was told to give the two spirals to Joan as a symbol of protection.

She relayed all of this information to Joan and let her know that the golden disc and the two spirals were signs that she needed to take away with her, in order to heal. She also called her guides into her plane of existence and asked them to help her clear Joan's space. She rattled around her to make sure that her energy was balanced. She took her palms, blew sharply into them to cleanse them and drew and imprinted the waterfall spirals into her palms. She pressed her palms together to seal the sacred energy into her being and placed her palms on her heart so it would integrate into her body.

The ancestral healer observed that considering the theme and the reason for healing it was good to see that the client was in good spirits throughout the session. She was smiling a lot and said she felt lighter at the end of the session. She was also jovial and found humour in much of what was discussed. Two days later, the healer checked in with Joan and she said she was feeling nauseous the morning after the session, but that all of this had been very positive and she was now feeling less anxious.

Influence of Ancestral Healing on Illness

Ancestral healing is the key to getting to the origin of an issue and to transforming it and energetically healing the whole ancestral field of this repeating pattern. To work effectively, training as an ancestral healer is required and also having the ability of expert divination skills. There are many factors that have created distortion in the genes and illness down through the generations.

I have listed a selection of improvements clients felt after ancestral healing.

Ancestral Healing

Trait to be healed	Experience of trait after ancestral healing
Distrust towards other people	Have entered new relationship and issues have healed
Blocked spiritually and creatively	Connected to creative gifts, now painting and working as a Shamanic Healer
Sexual abuse of children in many generations, experienced by the client herself	Feels this experience has healed, less angry, not afraid to be herself
Lack of confidence	Feels more confident
Loneliness connected to mother's feeling of loneliness	Feels less lonely and connecting more with other people
Addiction problems	Feels freer to connect to the spiritual path, some addictions cleared
Non-communication with sister, feelings of isolation and guilt	Back in communication with sister, more feelings of joy
Feared father due to cultural environment	Better communication with father, feels less oppressed
Persistent skin problems	Cured after ancestral healing
Depression	Cured after ancestral healing
Did not speak to father	Now in good communication with father
Trauma, raped as a young woman, self-harm	No longer self-harms
Constant negative thought forms	More feelings of joy

DNA Scripts

Junk DNA does not code for protein, but it does code for a different kind of molecule RNA. A major role of junk DNA is to regulate gene expression.

Ancestral Genetic Scripting Healing Exercise

Write your present Ancestral Genetic Script that needs to be healed in 20 words. Include six words that are a negative expression of your source self, such as: fear; depression; sadness. From the negative experiences of your ancestral lineage.

Focus on one pathway: your mother's or father's ancestral lineage in one expression.

For example, from my father's ancestral lineage of violence, I have created a life of fear, distrust, lack of empathy, apathy, isolation, violence.

Fill in your script below.

DNA Script inherited from Ancestral Mother Lineage

_____

_____

_____

_____

_____

DNA Script inherited from Ancestral Father Lineage

_____

_____

_____

_____

_____

_____

Now, rewrite your DNA script in the same format. Replacing the negative words with positive words. For example from my mother's side I have a life of joy, abundance, empathy, love, power and strength.

Light a candle and state that you release the negative DNA script, release it to the fire of the candle. State aloud the positive DNA scripts that you bring to yourself. Continue this as a mantra every day for 10 days to allow this to embed in your energetic field.

Ancestral Wisdom

Illness provides a road map for the explanation of pain. It is contained within our bones and that of our ancestors, the hidden knowledge, which explains the wisdom of before. The journey to wellness is one that needs to be carried out by delving into the soul. The soul template contains memory of all that is; our wounds; and our ancestor's wounds. There are seeds of information that need to be explored, which hold the possibility of seeding a new reality. Delving into energy and time will provide a picture of the story, which is often of conflict. The conflict contained within the self is manoeuvring to clear the story that exists. This is connected to the illness that we display, which is a reflection of what has gone before.

Within everyone's container of ancestral lineage and wisdom are the stories of trauma, along with the opportunity to delve into the origins of where the pain and distortion started that created the illness. It did not start with our parents; it started many years before that. Healing ancestral illness at its origin, paves the way for a future generation that is able to let go of the pain of ancestral illness and the restrictions this holds. It frees aspects of the DNA to embrace new changes, which can bring more positive change and soul evolution.

The dove is a symbol of peace and harmony. There is hope for everyone. When we enter into turmoil it is to help heal the conflict within. Peace comes in many forms and the many forms we can access. It simply takes the right fuel and ignition to get back to peace and health in your life. Illness can be seen as a trigger point to reconnect the trauma of the past that has come up for healing, to heal the past, present, and future for yourself and your ancestors. When we are free of pain, we are freeing the pain of the human life on earth. Repeated illness and patterns reflect repeated pain contained within the ancestral field. The signs are there to observe and release.

Reflection time

*Write your insights, healing and tasks moving
forward to continue to heal your life.*

Chapter 9

Ancestral Lands: Inherent Foundations of Wisdom

Energetic imprints in the ancestral lands are woven together, to bring into being our connection from the past for the future.

Memories of the Past

At our origins we are all connected to the one ancestor. Our mother and father may be from a particular land but beyond that in the ancestral lineage, there are many connections to many lands. When we embrace this concept, there is less separation among humans. The universe organises and aids the birth of different nations and different tribes, all with a role of helping to mould the consciousness on Earth. How they aid the consciousness of the earth is how they connect with nature and everything around them. A disconnection from nature creates a disharmonious flow between nature and humans and problems can be created, which affect the internal and external landscapes. The ancestral land connection is related to many generational memories. Animals and humans walk the land, and a connection is made to many ancestral generational memories and energy is contained in the stones and nature that reside there. These all hold memory, as do the bones of the ancestors who are buried in the land.

The internal landscape mirrors the external landscape. Memory is symbolic of connection. When there is connection to ancestral land, there is an ability to mirror the soul and to be reminded that all is connected. The land shapes and moulds the energy of the landscape and the individual. It serves as a connection to help heal and transform everything within everything. Humans are transient and move and live in different lands. However, the choice of when to leave a land has often not been given, nor has the opportunity to return. Many lands have been taken away dramatically and immorally and given to other people or sold for money or for personal gain. Wars have displaced communities and forced them to lose their connection with their ancestral lands. This creates turbulence which never settles on the lands affected, the ancestors wailing in pain over their divine inheritance, which has been taken away, wandering the landscape at times in disharmony.

It is important that choices are given to those people who occupy land. It is traumatic to be pulled away dramatically from a land and a land taken away with no opportunity to return. The dramatic move away from ancestral lands leads to a loss of connection, which is an important imprint to have. Imprints of memory of different lands serve to reconnect with gifts, wisdom, and ancestral knowledge. The energetic fields of ancestral lands become distorted, if not used in ways that are connected to their inherent nature. This disconnection does not serve those who dwell there. The energetic field of the land needs to be in harmony with those people who occupy the land.

When humans move from land to land, the essence of the land is carried with them. Memory is placed and contained with the energetic landscape of the lands. Often pilgrims follow these footsteps to places of sacred power. Rituals are held in those places and sometimes memory is placed there to help the future. Buildings may collapse and be rebuilt, but energetic memory remains as an imprint in memory.

Land Karma

Karma in the context of land, relates to when there has been an event that has transformed the ancestral land in a negative way. This can be by fracking on sacred sites or bloodshed causing the displacement of inhabitants. It may also be by the misuse of land by those who occupy it, or the use of the land for dark arts to harm other people. This can affect those people who live on the land because it affects consciousness and attracts that which it is associated with. What has gone before feeds into this consciousness and the energy attracts particular thought forms, which continue to feed into humans who occupy the land in the future. The aim has always been to be in harmony with the land by those people who reside on it. Many lands have been misused in many ways. On many lands there has been mass trauma and as a result there are karmic imprints in the land, which have continued down the generations.

The rise in capitalism and the power and value of land ownership have resulted in many events that have shattered communities and the energetics of lands. In many countries there has been a considerable building of high-density property, leaving little space to create natural spaces in nature and little space for nature to provide harmony and balance.

Ancestral lands contain rivers of information which is why many pilgrims travel to sacred sites. It has always been this way. Lands seed truths for the future and energetic practices enable shifts in consciousness by connecting energy and sounds to landscapes. Energetic practices by indigenous people were created from the wisdom gained by nature. They worked with nature and the spirits around them, to create processes to heal and transform their communities, these processes have been passed down generations. The ancestors are able to connect to lands for wisdom, to help their lands and their children. Many ancestral lands carry many rivers of blood and trauma that have left the land shattered. Inevitably, as consciousness and energy shifts on the planet, the lands are returning to their natural energy. The energy is shifting to seed new information for the future to help the planet in positive ways.

The lands that we inherit are there to serve and to enable a connection, which is harmonious. These lands provide the food; our foundation and all that humans need to exist. Many lands have been desecrated and used in dark rituals, these rituals attract in energies that can disconnect with the harmonious forms of energies. This feeds in thought forms of fear, power abuse, and harming other people. This creates a polarity among people who are attracted to these energies and those who are not. It fragments communities and can instil fear, control, and power abuse. This leads humanity backwards not forwards, the reverse being that working harmoniously with the land creates harmonious communities.

The ancestors of the land are left without their anchorage of what is harmonious and what is part of their nature. This also breaks away energetic support from the land. The land does not work at a similar level anymore, because those who move to occupy it, often have no interest in connecting energetically to the land, nor receiving the support the land provides. The same stones and plants may be there but this distortion causes an energetic change to plants and stones, which may become vibrationally lower. Purpose and vision are what the ancestral lands are about, providing a direction which rewards those who align with the land energy. For those people who create disharmony with the land, the land can sometimes take away what has been given.

Ancestral Land Wisdom

Ancestors, particularly indigenous ancestors, employed techniques that worked directly with the land, which held all the wisdom that was needed. In certain circumstances the land displayed energies to show the power contained within it. The ancestors transmitted this to work with. This kept an interplay between the ancestors and nature. This interplay was kept as a memory in the earth and this wisdom was conveyed to other people by the spoken word and also by the land to those who connected with it. It has always been the case that wisdom is carried through the land in fields of energetic wisdom. This allows ancestors to access the inherent wisdom, which provides knowledge for the future. Wisdom keepers are there to ensure that this wisdom carries through time and helps to serve the ancestors who follow. If this wisdom is used for the good, it can have a divine power to heal and transform. This wisdom is important because it provides memory of healing and transformation. This can go as far back to the original ancestor and contained within this is wisdom of the past for the future.

Grids of light are contained within the land. These are activated by ancestors and other people who are able to help this light connect to the earth. There are points in the earth, which at certain times will be activated to aid the earth. Ancestor connection is embracing all the beliefs in harmony that embrace everyone. A wave forms together to symbolise the oneness of the soul and of the ancestors. The collective ancestors are coming together with the holders of wisdom to help orchestrate a reconnection with the earth again. Many ancestors who now live away from their ancestral lands are reawakening to their inherent knowledge and wisdom, and thus to the importance of reconnecting with and preserving this wisdom and nature again.

Wisdom is built on another person and transformed and more wisdom stacked on top. This helps to build new foundations for the future. Translation of wisdom acts to drive inspiration and courage to build on. The spirits of the land have connections to particular lineages which forms particular foundations or spiritual beliefs. This is harnessed in the land by particular rituals or ceremonies from our ancestors through which we will also obtain this knowledge. Nature provides the foundation for everything, without it there would be no energy transference of ancestral wisdom. Transference from nature transforms; evolution cannot take place without it. Sacred awareness serves to translate the wisdom that is hidden to those ancestors who can use it at the right time.

Ancestral Lands and the Divine Inheritance

We can say that the earth is one huge ancestral land. The importance of ancestral land is a divine inheritance to aid connection. It is also important for humanity to respect the power that is harnessed there.

Ukraine

Arrata developed north of the Black Sea, in what is known now as modern Ukraine. Like many ancestral lands there exist landmarks and sacred sites to mark and show the energetic points of the land. One landmark is Kamyana Mohyla, which is a mound consisting of large sandstone slabs on a hill above southern Ukraine. It has a number of grottoes and many Palaeolithic petroglyphs, which serve as references to man's earliest myths.

Ancestral Story
Ukraine and matriarchal society

Sofia was brought up by a Ukrainian mother and Mongolian father in the Ukraine. She discussed the essence of the land, its influences, and the effect on her. Her father and his family lived a nomadic lifestyle across Russia and Poland. Her grandfather was a high ranking general who fought in World War Two and who was of Mongolian descent. During his time in the army, he experienced separation from his culture and people. This affected Sofia's father deeply because he felt no sense of belonging and no sense of family. He therefore followed in his father's footsteps and joined the army, but later became a police sergeant and travelled around with no permanent base or home. He was a sensitive soul who loved people, nature and animals and above all wanted to help everyone and treat everyone fairly. However, he was constantly trying to survive and other people tried to trick him and take advantage of him. He became very disappointed and deeply depressed becoming an alcoholic. Many years later he died of alcoholism.

Sofia's family worked mainly with agriculture; they learnt the importance of treating nature with love and how nature gives back. The history of her ancestral lineage connected to the Ukraine had plenty of trauma. This made the ancestors and herself and her family strong and united together in the darkness. They learnt to share the good experiences with each other. She felt that the land is ever forgiving and evolving, carrying immense power of regeneration. It carries ancient knowledge, as well as the blood and bones of her ancestors. She knew that to really understand herself she needed to know her family history and roots. Suffering and joy were part of these experiences.

Sofia's mother was born in the time of war. All her mother's family were farmers and owners of land. They had no wealth but lived mainly on the land. Sofia's great grandmother was a healer and followed a healing tradition of the land and practised these rituals in secret. After the war, the Soviet occupation took the family land and made it their communal land. This left the family with nothing to eat and they had to find work elsewhere. These were miserable times, where they looked for scraps of food to eat, often finding no food at all. As they were patriotic and not wanting to belong to communist Russian regime many were sent to Siberia to prison and held as political prisoners. Her grandfather spent 10 years in prison and her grandfather and uncle were imprisoned and never released. The women and children were spared. The women were strong, providers and protectors. They turned their attention to study and *many of them went to university. Sofia's grandmother was a single mother with two small children; she educated them and also educated them into the knowledge of the land and ancient culture. She had an extremely hard life, but was extremely strong and proud and even at 80 years old, Sofia said she could feel the power of her presence and kindness, Sofia's mum was a single mum of two girls. The hardships they had experienced hardened her and made her fearless; however she had the most forgiving and compassionate of hearts. She continued to follow her culture and be true to herself. Sofia was proud to have inherited this feminine power, which runs deep within her and the ancestral influences of both the Ukrainian and Mongolian sides of her lineage. She is a nomad who has travelled the world and seen many cultures.*

As a Ukrainian, she carries a tradition of her race, influenced by the land of Arrata and its ancient wisdom. Ukraine continues to be a matriarchal society. The women were priestesses, healers, and heads of families. Sofia now works as a healer too. She is proud of her healing and spiritual work. Along with caring for the children, the women also made important decisions concerning the family and community. During the early times there was great respect for each other and from nature. Even after the conversion to Christianity, females were held in high respect and were leaders of their homes. Many healing practices were prosecuted by the church, so many people practised in secret. However, the healers have continued today and it is common to go to the 'babka' or old crone. Coming from a strong feminist family, this strong feminist energy runs deep in Sofia, she is proud of this feminine energy. She felt immense gratitude and love for her ancestors.

Sofia's message to the world is that the ancestral land offers you everything, including: the story and understanding; the healing and love; the opportunity to forgive and a space to forgive. The ancestral lands need to be honoured with respect and love.

Aboriginal Land; Inherited Past

The land of Australia has been occupied for a very long time by the aboriginal tribes. This has left a significant memory in the earth that can be used for the present, as well as the future.

Aboriginal Wisdom

It is well known that the ancestors in northern Australia had ancestors who occupied these lands for tens of thousands of years. Tom Ebury–Dennis, in his article, *"Indigenous Australians Most Ancient Civilisation on Earth"*, in the Independent Newspaper online, discussed how scientists completed research into DNA in the modern Australian population. They found that their origins date back more than 50,000 years back to the Stone Age. This shows an ancient culture with ancient wisdom.

The author, Ashley Montagu in his book, *Coming into Being Amongst the Aboriginals,* researched the Aboriginal Arunta tribe of central Australia, who had an important connection to the land of their birth. Aboriginals generally speak of themselves, the area they live in or inhabit and often give descriptions of themselves by animals or plants, believing that every animal and plant has a representative among human inhabitants. They believe that whenever an ancestor came to the earth, there would be a sign of this entrance represented by, for example a tree, rock or waterhole. This tribe therefore, had a strong and harmonious connection to the land and animals around them, which is called totemic. They have spiritual emblems inherited by members of a clan or family. These totems help to define their roles and responsibilities with each other and all of creation. The importance of the connection to the land of their birth is very important.

There is a strong kinship among aboriginal tribes and this shapes behaviour towards not only their own kin, but to society in general and towards other groups and tribes. The relationship between parent and child is described as a social group; they acknowledge the importance of relationship not only from biological relationship, but also from sociability. Ashley Montagu explained how the Alchera tribe, who were direct ancestors of the Arunta tribe, created various natural features of the land inherited by the tribe. The land continues to speak to various indigenous cultures and conveys the wisdom of their ancestors.

These strong ties to land and culture created harmonious conditions of self and culture. Many researchers are now realising the importance of connecting directly with indigenous people to obtain wisdom and stories of their ancestors. George Nicholas in his article, "After Thousands of Year's Western Science is Slowly Catching up with Indigenous Knowledge" for *Yes* magazine, describes how researchers in northern Australia were researching kites and falcons and the behaviour of "Intentionally carrying burning sticks to spread fire". Birds can also be known for this behaviour because this causes reptiles, insects, and rodents to move to other areas. This creates an opportunity for the birds to be freer to search for food. This behaviour by nighthawks was a new discovery by scientists. They found that this was already known by the Malak, Jawoyn and other indigenous peoples of northern Australia, as it was ancestral knowledge that had been passed down the generations. Scholars and scientists are becoming aware of the vast amount of traditional and indigenous knowledge that is available to aid research into the past.

The ancestral lands give birth to continuous knowledge to help humanity. The Nyangkari's are aboriginal healers of the Anagu of the Western Dessert in central Australia, which is the name given to spirit healers. This wisdom of healing has been passed down the generations. The healers work with plants, animal products, spiritual healing, dance, and song to heal patients. Massage is also sometimes used as part of the healing practice. They have knowledge of plants from around the areas they live and these plants are used to heal other people. For example, the desert fuchsia is used to heal and to treat chest infections. Recent studies by scientists have identified antibacterial compounds found in the desert fuchsia. The healers believe that to heal a person, the person has to be approached spiritually and physically. Georgina Kenyon, in her article, "Australia's Other Flying Doctors", for *Mosaic* in 2016, discussed how; Francesca Panzironi, an independent researcher is convinced that: "The Nyangkari's are needed to bring down the high rates of mortality amongst indigenous people". This is an interesting concept and shows the importance of reconnecting traditional healing ways, with an indigenous community. The ancestors knew what was needed to heal and this is aligned with the genetic constitution of what is right for an individual.

There are many organisations trying to help the documentation of this wisdom to preserve Aboriginal wisdom. However, most Aboriginal communities' experiences have been of severe discrimination and living way below the poverty line and disconnected from their ancestral lands.

Trauma

Like many indigenous people throughout the world many of the Australian Aboriginal tribes were displaced from their homes and social groups. There was the stolen generation, when tens of thousands of Australian Aboriginal children were deliberately removed from their families between 1910 and 1970. The children particularly mixed-race children, were sent to various camps in different parts of Australia. The aim of this strategy was to assimilate them into white Australian society. However, these were desperate conditions with poor sanitation, high rates of illness, and premature death. The removal of children continued for more than half a century and it is well known that much of this complex civilisation was wiped out by 1860, when the land was divided up by Europeans. The Indigenous people were cultivating and preserving the soil as well as sea life, using their own Aboriginal agriculture skills and the ancestral land also suffered as a result of their displacement. Lorena Allam, in her article for *the Guardian* online, wrote about the high suicides among the Aboriginals in 2019; "There were 35 dead in 3 months, including a 12- year old, this is higher than the average amongst non-aboriginal groups."

Ancestral Story
Channelled wisdom from the Aboriginal collective

I have strong Aboriginal guides and a past life as an Aboriginal. I am strongly connected to this lineage. I channelled directly from the aboriginal consciousness to share their message.

> *"Treading the earth, we were able to tap into the collective wisdom that guided consciousness. When we came into being, we connected directly to the chord that binds with the earth consciousness. Our beliefs were aligned with what was required for a harmonious earth. Delving into matter,*

we were able to explore different strands of consciousness and also listen to what creation had to say. The stars also guided us, which reflected man's inner truth.

Memory is the key to helping the future. Contained within every gram of the earth is the memory of all that exists. To reverse what is malfunctioning on the planet, gain entry to the memory of the earth. Do not discount what has gone before; activate this again for flow to return to the planet. Plants hold the balance for everything, they are connected to all aspects of reality and they stand firm on the ground and receive the wind and air. They communicate in two ways to feed what is below and what is above; both are important to achieve balance. Plants need to be close at hand to help the environment and allow harmony to take place in the chaos.

Human nature caused us pain and non-acceptance. Treated like misfits, we were cast out from our lands. We lost our way because we were disconnected from what had guided us and in many ways our wisdom became fragmented. Sounding from the heart and mind creates an energetic field that is able to manifest and create. Explore this concept and see how this plays out in helping the present and the future. Discrimination serves no purpose and it disempowers and creates separation. In the future man-made errors will cause disaster to human form. To minimise the energetic damage to the environment, make it alive again, allow it to sing its song together in harmony. This will enable transformation and resurrect of what has been buried for too long.

The wisdom we can gain from this ancestral land is the connectedness between man, plants, and nature. This creates harmony between groups and culture. It also creates conditions to provide information on ways *to heal and how the plants around us can be used for healing and this wisdom passed down to other people."*

Native American; Ancestral Lands

The Native Americans occupied many lands and their indigenous teachings and ways of being demonstrated how to be in harmony with the land. From this relationship they received all that they needed.

Wisdom

Native American teachings believe that everything is related and this was incorporated into everyday practices and ceremonies. In the Sioux tradition, it was the sacred women who bore the gift of the pipe. The pipe represented male and female, it also symbolised the acceptance in the system of relatedness that comprises the universe, creating a harmonious relationship between man and the spirits. The Native Americans are deemed to have common ancestors in the Sioux tradition and view this kinship as an act of relating. They recognised that we are all related and part of a common wisdom. There is a powerful Sun Dance that normally happens once a year, this is a Prayer dance, and the message is suffering to sacrifice. In this ceremony, which normally lasts four days, it is not only the individual who participates but also the rest of the tribe and the universe. The ceremony is to honour all of life and what sources life, for renewal and regeneration.

From birth, Native Americans were brought up to have a strong connection with animals, plants and children were often named after a plant or animal. Earth is understood as a temple and as a result it is treated with utmost respect. Prayers, ceremonies and rituals were conducted to maintain a harmonious relationship with all that lives around them. This is a beautiful concept which all of humanity can aim for. All of creation are felt to have spirits, including rocks, plants, and animals.

Different cycles of nature are honoured with ceremony; prayers and offerings are given to plants and animals to help create a harmonious relationship and as a thank you for their use. Children are brought up to respect animals, even the more dangerous ones. They are also taught not to waste anything that had been harvested. They are in tune with the growing cycles of nature and knew the best times to harvest. As described by author M. Kat Anderson, in her book *Tending the Wild*, she described how Indian narratives stated that; "Humans were given specific instruction through the spirit world to protect the earth's self–replenishing character".

Trauma

In the article, *"Rethinking Historical Trauma"*, for Sage Journals, Laurence Kirmayer and company discussed how: "The persistent suffering of the indigenous people in the Americas reflects not so much past trauma as on-going structural violence." Over time, settlers have suppressed Native American traditions and also moved native people away from their native lands to boarding schools and used strategies to marginalise them from each other. In the article, "Native Americans, Past, Present and Future", William J Szlenko and other authors, discussed how: "Native Americans have higher rates of alcohol use and increased rates of fetal alcohol syndrome, compared to other ethnic groups". Before colonisation alcohol was not known to Native Americans; explorers introduced alcohol in exchange for various goods; and as a means to show kinship and friendship. Colonisation also created a collective trauma by introducing alcohol as a means to control other people and as a bargaining tool. This influence on their culture and the affect on the ancestral lineage have been proven to move down and influence the ancestral generations. Introducing something that was not familiar to a culture causes a distortion in the energy field and consequently an illness manifesting to the ancestors. Escapism does not allow the body to feel pain or remember. Traditional indigenous healing methods that may have been implemented to heal or manage these illnesses were sometimes put aside when the distraction of alcoholism came into play. The memories of these healing methods were lost, creating more distance from their natural profound wisdom and knowledge.

Ancestral Wisdom;
Channelled wisdom from the Native American collective

I have many Native American guides and have a past life as a Native American. The following words are channelled directly from them:

"Destiny is in the hands of humanity. For a long time, nature connection and indigenous people were leading the shifts in wisdom all over the world. This period of time has been taken away, along with many opportunities for this knowledge to be accessed. Birds speak to each other to negotiate and play. Humans in many ways have lost their voices and interplay with each other. Native Americans used movement and dance to connect to the creative dance of the universe and to aid this connection, every movement held connection with the universe. Ancestral lands hold our traditions and many people are destroying this, which not only displaces the indigenous tribes but creates disturbance in the energetic fields of those people who are connected to this lineage. Displacements shake the earth. The earth is a creative force and its foundations are built on energy gateways and portals to allow memory to be obtained.

Native people always speak of harmony to smooth through differences that man may have created. Reflection is not corrupted when we reflect back to each other in harmony. There is really no other way to move forward. When we connect consciously on the earth, we immediately connect with our soul. We feel its energy which helps us to live our lives. Without this connection, it would be hard to create all that we make in the world. In oneness we aid the truth of who we are.

What man does to be so called 'forward thinking' actually reverses in terms of energetic movement of the planet. In our dreams we are able to connect to the consciousness of the earth. It held us in its heart; it allowed the ancestors to grow and through time we were able to see signs from the stars above and the land helped shape our beliefs. Turmoil in man in many ways allows a focus on what is available to activate. This has a hand in creating a large void and the gap in separation kills the joy that many people had. The inherent nature is to stand hand in hand, with the ancestors and families, who lived together in a tradition that served one another and nature in a harmonious way. To many people this wisdom has been lost."

Effects of Ancestral Land Trauma

As migrant people we move from land to land, but the effect of dramatically being pulled from ancestral lands is a huge trauma for the land and the people affected and has huge effects as described below.

1. Abandonment
    *   Not being protected, not feeling safe and a sense of loss.
    *   These feelings create a fear of being let down or abandoned by other people.

2. Separation from ancestral land
    *   Feelings of loss.
    *   Ancestral lands hold many memories and connections, when dramatically disconnected from ancestral lands there is a feeling of not feeling at home anywhere.

3. Soul loss
    *   Soul loss for people separated from their families, particularly children.
    *   Soul loss creates fragmentation of the soul, when parts of the soul feels scattered.
    *   While the journey of the soul continues, there are parts of the soul that are yearning to return.

4. Anger
    *   Angry feelings towards self and other people.
    *   Possible aggressive behaviour as the result of anger.

5. Illness
    *   Manifestation of illnesses such as depression.
    *   Suicide tendencies.

6. Nature
    *   Reducing activity of nature.
    *   Less space for nature to grow.
    *   Less use of nature to heal.

Ancestral Rituals to Heal Ancestral Lands

Rituals are powerful and they work to bring love and harmony to the ancestral lands, which need healing.

1. **Ritual for the ancestors' lands; healing the trauma of the land.**
    This ceremony is to honour your ancestors who have been traumatised on their ancestral lands. Do this in turn, separately for your mother and father. You do not need to be physically on the ancestral land, there is no time and space and the healing and energy will connect to the land that is requested.

    Take a glass of water. Hold it and state that you honour the ancestors who have gone before and their ancestral lands. As you hold the water, intend for it to be infused with the energy of harmony and love. Ask that this harmony and love go to the lands of your ancestors, to bring harmony and peace for your mother or father lines. You can state which specific lands you want this to go to. Pour the water onto the land, tap three times with your flat hand on the ground and state; "It is done". This allows the energy of the water to connect to where it is needed.

2. **Ritual to connect to the wisdom of ancestral lands.**

    Connect to your heart. Ask to connect to the ancestral lands for your mother's or father's side that holds the highest gifts for yourself. Ask your heart to show you these gifts and how these can be used to help yourself and other people. Write these down and ask them to be embraced within you. Thank your mother's or father's line for the gifts from the past for the future.

Ancestral Wisdom

Disconnecting from the indigenous wisdom connected to our ancestral lands is disconnecting from our ancestors and ourselves which forms part of our bloodline. The lands speak to us with a wisdom that is contained within. If we lose our connectedness with the land we inherit, or from the land on which we live, we lose the opportunity to be connected to an energy force that is there to embrace and support.

Anthropologists and scientists are recognising the importance of indigenous and ancestral wisdom as an important way of connecting to ancient wisdom. We need to support the indigenous people who continue to live on the earth, as the wisdom keepers of great ancestral wisdom. This is needed to prevent the earth from 'falling apart' and being an uninhabitable planet for humans and animals. Aligning with the land and nature is the key to communicating with an innate wisdom that can aid and support all who inhabit it.

The ancestors walked many lands before us. They gathered wisdom in abundance for healing and living in harmony with the land. They helped pave a great future that helped nature and the future generations. The creative force of nature is what binds together communities, and losing this connection creates separation from nature and from each other. Our indigenous ancestors taught us the importance of harmony and connection. For many people a pilgrimage to ancestral lands will serve as a way of reconnecting with aspects of their gifts, and this will aid the strengthening of our inherent nature. The importance of honouring the ancestors and their lands that have gone before us awakens an energetic force of connection.

Ancestors are being driven from their lands or being displaced for money, discrimination, or power. Displaced in these dramatic ways, displaced people lose the anchorage of a land of support that has given them wisdom and allowed them to be in harmony and balance. This causes trauma and inevitably affects future generations, leading to feelings of disempowerment and fragmentation.

Pathways of consciousness via experience are there for a reason; they each have teachings for the soul. What we have experienced leads us to greater wisdom and knowledge. What we explore turns the point to our awakening. Give or take, we need to mirror ourselves with the ancestors. When we reflect, we will know what the ancestral lands have to teach us, each day and every day, in every moment.

There are many gifts that have been gained from our ancestors and the lands of the ancestors, including ancient wisdom that can help with healing and help the earth. Ancestral lands hold great wisdom. The lands where there has been the most trauma affect the ancestors now, and understanding this helps heal ancestral patterns and illness. Every space and land has a story; beneath it holds the mystery that has the ability to transform. Place yourself in that story and allow what you hear or see to unfold and what changes are needed in your life, to gain great renewal of self.

Chapter 10

Gifts from the Ancestors: Celebrations of Divine Inheritance

*Travelling through time, seeds were sown
to gift future generations.*

Ancestral Gifts

Ancestral gifts are memories and information contained within the collective and DNA. This is to ensure that these gifts and wisdom remain in the ancestral fields and are passed down the generations. They provide memory of what has been seeded before to create positive harmonics of life in the ancestral field, so this connection can continue to provide a great existence. We celebrate this connection of what was seeded for future ancestral generations by past ancestral lineages. Ancestral gifts enable the ancestor to navigate and connect with them. Imagine this connection being like a tunnel, there is an opening somewhere and an exit. It is the same with accessing ancestral gifts, there is an entrance point; an opportunity to connect with these gifts that are sacred and available; and to exit with these gifts at any time.

Our gifts are a platform to express our inherent nature, which needs to be expressed because it is part of the ancestral lineage. When we truly express who we are, we live in harmony and joy. Denying the positive aspects of the self leads to limitation and other negative factors. Connecting with the positive aspects, allows flow and connection. Ancestral gifts are here to remind us of our ancestors in a positive way. They also provide signposts to what can make a difference to individuals and the lives of other people. There are positive attributes that are contained within the DNA, which provide inherent qualities that positively influence. DNA contains memory from both our mother's and father's ancestral lineage and this is highly protected within the consciousness of the DNA. Through the different journeys and lifetimes, the ancestral imprints encode the energy field to provide useful and positive information. These can be accessed and used to provide gifts in different lifetimes.

Positive connections provide a harmonious link and harmony down the ancestral lines and allows for the ancestral connection to be embedded. Ancestral connection is not only about trauma and emotional turmoil; it is also about the positivity that the ancestral link brings to our lives. Waves of experiences create different waves of information, which are transmitted down the line. The soul plays these out during different lifetimes and so the inherited positive gifts continue down the generations it is the ancestor who chooses whether to connect to them or not.

Gifts allow imprints of positivity to be left on the earth and for future generations. This is not only invaluable for the individual but also for humanity as a whole. The individual also brings their own unique blueprint and gifts but they also inherit gifts from the ancestors on both sides of the families. Whether this is tapped into and used is down to free will. Ancestral gifts provide information that the earth can positively connect with, which helps the land and individuals. There are thousands of years and sometimes millions of years of information in our ancestral bones that contain great wisdom. The gifts that our ancestors leave can also be used to follow trails to sacred sites and lands. These can provide wisdom that has been left by the ancestor that humanity can tap into to help the earth.

How Gifts are Transmitted Down Generations

The eternal song of life exists in various ways down the ancestral line which is how information is transmitted. Our ancestors sang to connect us with ancestral ways, singing ancient songs of wisdom, transmitting vibrations in resonance with ancestors who received them. Songs of the earth are also available to provide and to aid that connection, along with healing songs to help other people. Word of mouth transmissions have been dying out for a number of years, so it is important to connect energetically with the ancestral lineage to enable reconnection because this wisdom is always available. The simple act of wanting to know and to connect provides the springboard to the connection to ancestral wisdom of the gifts that are waiting to be embraced and embodied.

Many languages are becoming extinct on the planet at a frightening rate and so is the loss of connection with the vibration, songs, ancestral memory, and resonance that this carries. Bob Holman describes in his interview on *PBS News Hour America*, in 2015 that many languages are disappearing and stated that: "If you lose the language, you lose that connection with that place, with that way of thinking, with tens of thousands of years of that language's lineage." On the same platform, it was also discussed how a song sung in a language called Amurdak, which the narrator described as; "a language spoken in Northern Australia. There is virtually only one person left on our planet who speaks Amurdak, his name is Charlie Mangulda". This is a language nearly gone from an Aboriginal community on Australia's Goulburn Island. Language is a gift from the ancestors that holds information, which needs to be preserved but many languages are falling away at a frightening rate.

Jeffrey Brown, senior correspondent and journalist for PBE stated that: "Predictions are dire that by the end of this century, more than half of the world's 6,000 languages will be gone".

The origins of our ancestral connection are within everyone. When we connect to gifts of the ancestors we are connecting to the origin of truth. Everything is protected and these gifts are beacons of light to show we have much to be proud of. As the ancestors return generation after generation, they celebrate when connection is made to their gifts and that their memories are upheld and preserved. Memory serves to mirror and reflect that which has gone before, it carries this transmission to other people. When we connect to ancestral gifts, it serves to align with memory that is contained within our DNA. This is always protected. It is up to the individual ancestor to embrace it or not.

Gifts are transmitted to ancestors born into a particular ancestral lineage. However, the activation of the embodiment of a gift can skip a generation. For example, it could be the granddaughter, not the mother, who connects with and chooses to activate and action the inherited gifts. With the inheritance of particular spiritual gifts, there is often the need for an ancestor to be born who is at a similar level of spiritual evolution, so they can take these gifts on vibrationally and energetically. Every avenue is taken to ensure that the gifts connect to the ancestors who are receptive and willing to uphold a tradition or spiritual gifts. However, often the ancestor can rebuke these. There is often a calling of the land for a particular soul to return who is needed for that community. With the activation of particular gifts, a soul can choose the place, the time, and the ancestral lineage that will ensure the receipt of these gifts. There may also be a need to be near to a soul group, that the soul chooses to be part of when the soul incarnates, to receive these gifts. Indigenous traditions and wisdom are often kept alive by this important factor.

Initiations

Initiations ensure that gifts are transmitted down the generations. A spiritual belief or shamanic tradition is often the accumulation of thousands of years of wisdom and knowledge passed down the generations. These can be given in the physical or spiritual forms. For example, in the Azande tradition training in the belief of witchcraft and practising can often start after a relative, such as a father or an uncle, choosing his relative to be in this tradition. They believe in training a child in their earliest years, as described by the author E. Evans-Pritchard, in his book *Witchcraft, Oracles and Magic Amongst the Azande*; "A novice begins to eat medicines with other witch doctors to strengthen his soul and to give him the powers of prophesy". This wisdom and knowledge remain in the DNA and is passed down the generations. The act of storytelling is also a way that wisdom is passed down the generations, along with initiations into traditions and healing practices.

The author Steven Feierman, in his book, *Social Basis and Health and Healing in Africa*, states that; "A diviner of the highest grade has ancestral spirits who speak directly to clients by whistling from the rafters of the house". These healers also have a variety of healing methods that they can use to help cure patients from an illness. These are amazing gifts that can be inherited from the ancestors.

In South Africa there are female healers called Inyangas. When they work, they enter into a trance to communicate with the spirits. If they have more advanced skills, they will use another method of divination by throwing bones. Within the DNA is this wisdom and knowledge, which is reactivated. On the reactivation is the support of the community and elders, who will help embed particular wisdom by storytelling and teaching the wisdom of the tribes.

Ancestral Story
Gift of healing, mother's side

Graham approached the ancestral healer to journey to connect with his ancestors, with a focus to connect to his mother's side. He wanted to ask his ancestors to come forth to share the gifts they have transferred to him and to ask how he could use them. When the ancestral healer connected to his mother's side, she began to smell a strong smell of smoke and saw a dark smokey cloud. The cloud of smoke was described by her spirits as a disease or disease of some kind. His mother's side had suffered very intense times of trauma, which had left them with disease manifesting as physical illness. The client's mother was going through a serious illness, during the time he came to the session.

During the session, the healer heard the word 'intuition'. Graham's ancestors were sharing with him the power of his intuition and that his gut feeling was communicating with him and he should follow this guidance. He also had the ability to see through smokey illusions beyond the here and now with great clarity. The ancestral healer had a vision of him as pure white light and to reach this light he had to follow the fire and passion in his stomach. During the session his Native Indian ancestors were keeping a light of support. His guide had a magnificent presence, his spiritual presence was helping to anchor him in the merging with his amazing spiritual gifts. The spirits were holding a space for him to embody these gifts and to bring them into the now. His ancestors stood proudly with the ancestor, who had chosen to embrace his spiritual gifts.

The ancestral healer also connected with Graham to help him to connect with his gifts on his father's line. While *connecting to his father's side, she immediately began to feel her physical body disintegrating to the beat of the drum. She was feeling and seeing the flow of energy as water and words that manifested were words such as 'flexible' and 'adaptable' and these words came strongly into her awareness. She dialogued with her guide and she questioned what was the ancestral gift on Graham's ancestral side. She observed that it was similar to his mother's side; gifts of energetic healing. She observed him using his hands over someone's body, moving energetic blockages, aligning the spine and sending in divine energy, all without physical touch. She felt the white light again and saw how he had the ability to merge with the energy of the other person and let his intuition guide him to clear energy. She advised Graham that once he was out of his self-identity and mind-level thoughts, he could deeply connect with energies. The ancestral session was out in nature and the healer kept receiving a thought about his birthday. When she asked him when his birthday was, he told her it was in a couple of days. He is a Virgo astrological sign, when they finished the session, they turned around to leave and on a broken log on the ground they saw the word 'VIRGO', carved into the log they were sitting next to. Graham thought possibly his ancestors were having a bit of fun and wishing him a Happy Birthday. He was full of joy that he had connected to his gifts on both ancestral lineages.*

Gifts for the Land

Ancestors come or return to particular lands to connect with particular tribes or ancestors who they choose at a soul level. Another reason can be to connect to particular sacred sites, to help leave information and wisdom for the present and future. Collectives of souls also come together at particular times on the earth to aid consciousness and to help the past, present and the future. In this context, ancestors leave gifts of consciousness that can help the earth and humanity. This is completed by, for example, the initiation of persons into traditions; the creation of new healers; work on sacred sites; and creating the guardians of ancient traditions for the future.

The lands are connecting the external and internal landscapes of the earth. External is what we see, internal is what is not seen by the naked eye. What we inherit helps to lay the foundations for the future, without it we would not know how to work with and cultivate the land. Whenever we connect to the land, we are leaving an imprint. Ceremony, ritual, and working with the land are all ways to connect with and create harmony with nature and this is left in the earth's memory. These are gifts from the ancestors leaving their imprints for other people to grow, learn, and work with.

Land holds the wisdom of everything that it connects to. This is important so humans remain connected to the wisdom of the land and the healing qualities it has to offer. Each depends on the other, even more so for remote tribes who depend on everything around them for their medicine, healing, and guidance. Animals that live on the land also leave their own imprints in the earth to help collective wisdom and evolution. When different tribes walked the earth they left their imprints and particular sounds and frequencies of energies in the earth. This allows a pathway of connection that other people can follow. Humans can automatically tap into guidance and support. This is the gift that the ancestors leave. Remaining open to the connections of land will enable humanity to have that connection.

Sacred sites are energetic anchors for the ancestors to connect to these energetic fields that feed us information and knowledge and leave many gifts. They are also signposts where other wisdom can be placed in the earth. These energetic containers help contain the energetic gifts and wisdom that cannot be destroyed by humanity. They are energetically open to those who are able to tap into this; and of course, bring through further wisdom and knowledge to help the future.

Star and Dragon Ancestors

There have been many incarnations of humans who are embodying star and dragon frequencies. Much has been written about the alignment of the pyramids in Egypt to Sirius and Orion. The star ancestors helped to create portals between the earth and the stars, creating a strong connection between the stars and the earth.

It was a way of anchoring energy on the earth. This ancestral wisdom from the stars is also anchored in the lands; particularly in sacred sites to help the earth and the individual's soul evolution. These ancestors worked to resurrect latent powerful energy that was already infused in the land. It needed a particular frequency to make this available again to help. Through different time periods, different humans were born on earth embodying particular star frequencies. Using sound and light they helped connect earth grids that activated energies to help the earth. Their wisdom was contained in their embodied star energy. Therefore, this wisdom contained the wisdom to help the earth to evolve and grow. The earth is a magnet of creation; the creative force that guides and shows the way for many people who can connect with it. The star ancestors enable more of the energetic fields to be open so more and more people can connect. With more people being in harmony with the earth it grows and evolves. These humans also help initiate other people into high source energy.

Dragons were involved in creating the earth; this archetypal energy is also embodied in some humans. Dragon ancestors had a role in creating pathways to help the land. Some individuals have ancestors who were dragons. These are archetypes of powerful energies involved in helping the earth's evolution. The dragons helped to connect many different gridlines of the earth so they worked together to enable connection of different lands and to help energy to connect where it was needed. The role of dragon energy was also to empower and to give strength to others and to help them move into mastery of who they are at a source level. They work powerfully with the earth during times of great energetic change.

Ancestral Story
Healer with sounds, mother's side

The ancestral healer worked with Claudette to help her to connect to the gifts on her mother's ancestral line. As the journey began, he saw Claudette around a fire and felt the presence of the jungle around both of them. He felt the presence of a deep ancient energy containing untold power. With this energy surrounding them, there was also a sound. The sound was subtle but this drew his attention and it had a prominent vibration.

Quickly, he saw Claudette transform and merge with the smoke of the fire, instantly transmuting and shifting to an extremely high frequency in a moment.

Here, he saw her on snowy mountain peaks, above them simply gliding through the clouds. She was singing with an incredibly strong, powerful voice but not using words, simple melodic sounds dancing between varying high tones. Though the sounds were simple, the vibrations were powerful beyond measure.

At this point he began to understand that the gift was related to her expression of sound, seemingly being able to share healing sounds through her voice.

In this image above the mountains she was wearing all white and surrounded by white energy, emanating a very powerful peaceful vibration. The sounds she was creating seemed to reverberate out across the planet in waves, sending healing to the earth and bringing balance to nature.

From the mountaintop she merged and shifted becoming a passing eagle soaring back down towards the earth. There was a discernible sound of the bird flying, but not the kind of sound the healer expected from the movement of the wings through the air. This again was like a vibration, a lower frequency oscillating with changes in the eagle's flight. This sound was a key part of the bird's ability to fly, not that the vibration was the source of the movement, but that the bird would not move in the same way without this precise frequency and vibration.

The image returned to the jungle. In it he saw Claudette communicating with different trees, plants and in particular a vine. She was humming and chanting in a soft quiet voice with deep to high tones, the plants were *moving joyfully in reaction and they were almost dancing together. Following on from this, he saw her with a white tiger, she calmed the tiger seemingly communicating with it and almost taming it with audible soft subtle sounds that again could not be discerned as words; almost mantra like, yet not a repetitive loop.*

The main attributes of this gift became clearer; the journey was showing her ability to transmit different frequencies through the sound of her voice. The journey also highlighted the importance of sound and vibration within this reality and its role in creation. She had the ability to connect easily with nature, plants and animals, working with the elements. It seemed that this gift included the ability to transmit the specific frequency of different actions or beings, to help heal other people. For example, the ability to channel and share the frequency of a specific herb for use in healing. Maybe this gift could evolve further beyond what could be currently comprehended to achieve other things, such as the levitation of objects with sound vibrations.

Ancestral Story
Master alchemist, father's side

The ancestral healer completed a shamanic journey to connect Ben with his gifts on his father's side. Soon after the drumming began the ancestral healer had stated her intention. She was greeted warmly by a guide of Ben's, an ancient spirit profoundly magical in nature with master alchemical abilities. Appearing as an older male wizard or alchemist, he was welcoming, loving, joyful and incredibly powerful. He quickly led the way into the lower realms, connecting with many different animals along the way including, wolves and boars, making themselves known and showing particular gratitude for the energy he was sharing.

The ancestral healer saw wilting plants regaining life simply from his presence. As they walked, he was moving energy with his hands and really enjoying this process of interaction with the energy around him. All of this seemed to show how easy it was for him to have a direct effect energetically with everything surrounding him.

They ventured deeper down into twisting tunnels to a space, which could only be described as the hell realms. The energy was much darker with a very eerie feel, potentially dangerous but the guide clearly had no fear and with him they felt completely safe and protected. There were many souls suffering and the feeling of a presence of dark forces controlling this space seemingly observing and feeding off the suffering happening here. The souls who were suffering were drawn to him and as they approached it was almost as if they entered a tunnel of light that allowed them to ascend from this realm and continue on their soul journey. His actions and demeanour brought about interesting lessons to be shared within this experience, particularly the importance of helping all of these different beings without any judgement.

Just before the end of the journey, they gradually made their way up out of the lower realms and returned to a peaceful setting in nature still in the spirit world, once again much like a jungle. Here, they were welcomed by familiar faces, one of them being Ben. As he joined them around the fire the wizard who had guided the ancestral healer, manifested food for everyone with simple movements of his hands.

There were many interesting factors to this journey. The ancestral healer did not see Ben clearly until right at the end, unlike the previous journeys where it felt as though the ancestral healer was observing him moving through realms. This time the guide, a higher aspect of himself, wanted to show the ancestral healer everything that Ben was capable of through his actions. It also felt important to recognise the difference in the general energy explored in each journey. Here they had ventured deep into dark realms where they were for most of the first journey and through his mother's line, they explored realities of a very high light. This showed how Ben could draw energy from both polar extremes, creating immense power from this dualistic balance that had a huge amount to offer right now in his density.

The gift the ancestral healer felt was presented throughout this journey could be described best as nothing less than pure master alchemical abilities. Showing that ultimately, matter in this reality can be manipulated in any way with absolutely no boundaries. It also showed the power that Ben could connect to and share is limitless because it came from a place of love with pure intention *and this could be used to help other people in all kinds of different circumstances.*

Barriers in Connection with Ancestral Gifts

In the ancestral lineage there are ancestors who do not work for the good of all and are happy at a particular aspect in time to remain this way. They can sometimes create problems in trying to stop an ancestor connecting with their gifts. This can create problems energetically, which can be very powerful and inhibiting. The ancestor needs to seek the appropriate help to ensure that these energies are moved away and more distant so they do not inhibit the person's path.

Another barrier to connecting to ancestral spiritual gifts could be that an ancestor rejects their energetic gifts maybe because of societal conditional, religious and family beliefs, or from not wanting to appear different. A person has free will whether they want to connect with their ancestral gifts or not and this needs to be respected.

Ancestral Story
Mediumship, mother's line

The ancestral healer completed a journey to the upper world to connect to the ancestor who would be sharing their gifts to help John on his path. Connecting to the aspect of time of the ancestor, the spiritual teacher guided the way. The ancestral healer heard the familiar whistle flute; the style of music she heard each time she completed her journeying for clients. She knew that she had made a connection with her spiritual teacher. She described the sounds from ancient Celtic Irish music being played through a wooden flute. She was from Irish descent. She heard the music playing through her left ear and passing across to her right ear.

As she approached the scene the ancestral healer saw beings dressed in long-hooded robes in a forest. All of a sudden, she saw arrows being shot in the direction of her spiritual guide. The ancestral healer felt scared and thought she was being deceived. She questioned her spiritual teacher to ask who he truly was and to show proof that he was genuine. The spiritual teacher told her in an urgent voice that they were under attack to prevent her from connecting John with the gifts from his maternal grandmother and great aunt. She quickly ran for cover, called on her spirit animals, and was guided to re-emerge once it was safe to do so.

It was dark in the forest even though she saw visibly, she couldn't see far. She knew her spiritual teacher was protecting her. She called on her spiritual guides to bring forward her spirit animals. All of a sudden, she heard a lion roaring, she saw a black panther roaming the forest, and had an eagle soaring above her. She saw dogs and cats everywhere. The dogs were sniffing the ground of the forest and the cats were there to shift the energy away from her. After that the ancestral healer didn't hear the arrows shooting anymore. She finally heard the tranquil and still surrounds of the forest. Almost immediately, she felt that John was connected to his grandmother and great aunt.

His grandmother and great aunt told the ancestral healer they are passing onto John their mediumship skills. John confirmed that he already had mediumship skills. The ancestral healer conveyed this message to the ancestors and they agreed that he already had the *gift of mediumship and that his abilities were good. They told her that John wasn't ready before to embrace more of this gift, whereas now his psychic and intuition abilities were clearer. From this connection, John had more faith in his abilities and himself and he felt ready to go on to strengthen his mediumship. John was also given information that he had the ability to give healing through his thumbs onto people's palms, which he wanted to explore more. The ancestral healer thanked her spiritual teacher and John's grandmother and great aunt and they said their farewells.*

Ancestral Ritual to Honour the Ancestors and Connect with Ancestral Gifts Exercise

Take time out in your life to honour the ancestors for your life and gifts. It is a great privilege to have a strong ancestral connection. It creates connection and respect. It also strengthens connection and guidance and this will help you to receive the guidance you need to connect to your ancestral gifts. Complete the ritual below in a quiet space with an open heart.

Light two candles, one to honour your father's side and one to honour your mother's side.

Say out loud the ancestral honouring prayer below.

Ancestral Honouring Prayer

The stars before me
The earth beneath me
The creative force that brought me into creation
The bloodline that brought me into being
I honour my father's line
I honour my mother's line
I choose my ancestral lineage
I honour them from afar and in the present
moment for giving me life
Your blood runs through my veins, it is the link that always connects
It always protects and guides
I send blessings and thanks to my ancestral line,
my mother and father and beyond
I seek forgiveness and hear their forgiveness
I reflect on my soul
It knows this cycle of life
I honour the cycle of life and give thanks
I set myself free from the chains that no longer serve me
I am a vessel to partake in any help that is needed
to support my ancestors at this time
I honour you all in all aspects of time
I call in the gifts of my ancestors to connect
I am grateful and thank you for your wisdom
And it is so
Thank you.

Spend some time in this space, receiving any wisdom or guidance, being in your heart.

Once you feel this is complete, allow the candles safely to burn out.

Breathe into your body and ground and centre yourself.

Ancestral Wisdom

Without the connection to our ancestors we cannot track important aspects of our souls. The gifts display memories that need to be preserved and embraced. This is important to lift consciousness to another level. However, the soul has many gifts from their own soul journey that aid soul evolution. If individuals and collectives of ancestors connected with the positive gifts down the ancestral line this would create a big shift in consciousness in a positive way. This would align with the positive attributes and help heal the negative aspects of ancestral connection. Positivity is always good for mind, body and spirit.

Being born into a particular ancestral lineage from your mother and father can distract from the fact that we have common ancestors. The different tribes who walked the lands before us and left their imprints of gifts for the earth are all energies that we are connected to. We may have been part of those tribes in past lives and these gifts are also in our DNA. The earth holds all the earth memories and when we walk the earth, particularly on ancient scared sites we automatically connect. Respect the land and nature because it allows access to our soul memory that is why it is so important to connect to the earth and protect the earth. It is important that we support indigenous people and healers because they are our roots; laying the foundations of thousands of years of wisdom that has been downloaded directly from spirits and nature. They help their communities to heal and transform. This is not old knowledge it is the wisdom that forms into the now.

We have ancestors in the stars, we are all stardust. They are real energies and many souls are embodying these energies here on Earth. These souls need to be supported with these gifts for the important work they have on Earth. This direct connection enables the channelling of information that is needed to help, along with the individual understanding more of who they are. It is the same for humans with ancestors who are dragon energies and who are embodying this on Earth. It is an important and powerful energy, which has a very powerful role in helping the planet it has done so over many years of the earth cycles.

There are many gifts contained within the mother's and father's ancestral lines, it is not only a lineage filled with distortions that have created illness and trauma. Ancestral lineages are also alive with stories of the joy of life and the wisdom that is contained within this. A soul has their own gifts from their soul journey but there are also inherited gifts to be accessed. By accessing these, it brings joy, connection with the ancestors, and alignment, and it is a person's divine right. Take time to connect with these gifts to enhance your life.

Contact the Author

The author can be contacted via email antheadurand@gmail.com

Or via her websites www.shamanismandevolvingconsciousness.com, www.antheadurand.com

Bibliography

Ainscough, Carolyn and Toon, Kay, *Surviving Sexual Abuse Workbook*, Da Capo Press, 2000

Allen, Sue, *Spirit Release, A practical handbook*, O Books, 2007

Anderson, Kat, M, *Tending the Wild: Native American Knowledge and the management of California's natural resources,* University of California Press, 2013

Bradford, Michael and Deerheart, Rosalie, *Soul Empowerment: A Guidebook for Healing yourself and Others*, Findhorn Press, 1997

Cohen, Anthony P and Rapport, Nigel, *Questions of Consciousness,* Routledge, 1995

Demallie, Raymond J and Ortiz, Alfonso, *North American Indian Anthropology: Essays on Society and Culture*, University of Oklahoma Press, 1994

Edinger, Edward F, *Anatomy of Psyche, Alchemical Symbolism in Psychology*, Open Court Publishing Company, 1985

Evans-Pritchard, Edward, *Witchcraft, Oracles and Magic amongst the Azande*, Oxford University Press, 1976

Feierman, Steven and Janzen, John, *Social Basis; health and healing in Africa*, University of California Press, 1992

Fiore, Edith Dr, *The Unquiet Dead, A psychologists Treats Spirit Possession*, Ballantine Books, 1995

Francis, Richard, G, *Epigenetics and how environment shapes our genes*, Norton Paperbacks, 2012

Gluckman, Max, *Custom and Conflict in Africa*, Barnes and Nobel, 1955

Glynn, Ian, *An Anatomy of Thought, The origin and machinery of the mind*. Oxford University Press, 2003

Gordon, Stuart, *The book of curses, the true tales of voodoo, hoodoo, and hex*, Citadel, 2000

Harmer, Harry, *Slavery, Emancipation and Civil Rights*, Pearson Education Limited, 2001

Hultkrantz, Ake, *Shamanic Healing and Ritual Drama, Health and Medicine in Native North American Religious Traditions*, Crossroads Publishing, 1997

Janzen, John, M, Nogoma, *Discourses in healing in central and southern Africa*, University of California press 1992

Kapferer, Bruce, *A Celebration of Demons, Exploration of Anthropology*, Berg Publishers, 1991

Kapferer, Bruce, *The Feast of the Sorcerer. Practices of consciousness and power*. University of Chicago Press, 1997

Laderman, Carol, *Taming the Wind of Desire, Psychology, Medicine, and Aesthetics in Malay Shamanistic Performance*, University of California Press, 1991

La Fontaine, Jean, *Child Sexual Abuse*, Polity Press, 1990

Lyon, William S, *An Encyclopedia of Native American Teachings*, William Lyon, 1996

Mack, Carol, *A Field Guide to Demons, Fairies and Fallen Angels and other subversive spirits*, Holt Paperbacks, 1999

Mead, Margaret and Calas, Nicholas, *Primitive Heritage, An Anthropological Anthology*, Random House, 1953

Meillassoux, Claude, *The Anthropology of Slavery – The Womb of Iron and Gold*, University of Chicago Press, 1992

Molyneaux, Brian Leigh and Vitebsky, Piers, *Sacred Earth Sacred Stones*, Duncan Baird Publishing, 2001

Montagu, Ashley, *Coming into Being Amongst the Australian Aborigines*, Routledge and Kegan Paul Limited, 1974

Ribi, Alfred, *Demons of the Inner World: Understanding our hidden complexes*, Shambhala publications 1990

Rose, Hillary and Rose, Steven, *Genes, Cells and Brains*, Verso books, 2012

Rupp, Rebecca, *Four Elements, Water, Air, Fire, Earth*, Profile books, 2005

Spierenburg, Peter, *Broken Spell, A cultural and Anthropolological History of preindustrial Europe*, Rutgers University Press, 1991

Turner, Victor W, *The Ritual Process, structure and anti–structure*, Transaction Publisher, 1995

Tyrrell, Barbara, *Suspicion is my Name*, T.V. Bullen, 1971

Tyrrell, Barbara, *Tribal people of Southern Africa*, Books of Africa, 1971

Van Dijk, Rijk, Reis, Ria and Spierenburg, Marja, *Quest for Fruition through Ngoma,Political Aspects of Healing in Southern Africa*, James Currey, 2000

Washington, Booker T, *Up from Slavery*, New York Doubleday, 1901

Notes

1. Dogon Tribe. Trinfinity and Beyond, by Kathy J Forti, June 7 2017, www.trinfinity8.com.

2. Health and Ancestors: The Case of South Africa and Beyond, by David Bogopa, November 2010 https://philpapers.org. Indo-pacific journal of phenomenology

3. Rethinking Historical Trauma, by Laurence Kirmayer, Sage journals 22 May 2014 https://journals.sagepub.com

4. Australia's Other Flying Doctors by Georgina Kenyon, Mosaic science, 5 April 2016 www.mosaicscience.com

5. Indigenous suicide: 35 dead in three months including three 12 year old children, by Lorena Allam, Guardian, 21 March 2019, Guardian online. www.guardian.com

6. Indigenous Australians most ancient civilisation on earth, by Tom Embury – Dennis, 22 September 2016 www.independent.co.uk

7. After thousands of years, western science is slowly catching up with indigenous knowledge, by George Nicholas 26 February, 2018, Yes Magazine www.yesmagazine.org

8. Native Americans, alcohol, past, present and future, by William J Lenko, James Woud and Pamela Jumper Thurman, 22 May 2014 for Journal of Psychology, www.researchgate.net

Made in the USA
Columbia, SC
08 January 2021